Exploring God's Word

by

Jack T. Parrish

Table of Contents

PREFACE

Searching for Pearls of Truth in the Scriptures

One of the most exciting things about immersing ourselves in the study of the Bible is the subsequent enlightening of our minds by the Holy Spirit. Jesus called Him the Spirit of Truth and said the Holy Spirit would remind His disciples of what Jesus told them about Himself and God's redemptive program.

- "But the Counselor, the Holy Spirit, whom the Father will send in my name, will teach you all things and will remind you of everything I have said to you." (John 14:26)

- "When the Counselor comes, whom I will send to you from the Father, the Spirit of Truth who goes out from the Father, He will testify about me." (John 15:26)

- "But I tell you the truth: it is for your good that I am going away. Unless I go away, the Counselor will not come to you; but if I go, I will send Him to you." (John 16:7)

- "I have much more to say to you, more than you can now bear. But when He, the Spirit of Truth, comes, He will guide you into all the truth. He will not speak on His own; He will speak only what He hears, and He will tell you what is yet to come. He will bring glory to me by taking from what is mine and making it known to you." (John 16:12-14)

True to the Lord's promise to His disciples, the Holy Spirit opened up the scriptures of the Old Testament to the disciples and enabled them to understand their meaning. Importantly, this new heavenly Counselor would not only dwell with the disciples, He would dwell *in* them, providing the power to be convincing, truthful witnesses of Jesus as God's Messiah.

- "But you will receive power when the Holy Spirit comes on you, and you will be my witnesses in Jerusalem, and in all Judea and Samaria, and to the ends of the earth." (Acts 1:8)

- "No, this is what was spoken by the prophet Joel: 'In the last days,' God says, 'I will pour out my Spirit on all people. Your sons and daughters will prophesy, your young men will see visions, your old men will dream dreams. Even on my servants, both men and women, I will pour out my Spirit in those days, and they will prophesy.'" (Acts 2:16-18)

Prior to the reception of the Holy Spirit, Peter did not have a clue what Joel's prophesy (above) meant. For a comparison of Peter's understanding of Old Testament scripture before and after the coming of the Holy Spirit, see his reaction to the Lord's statement about Himself – that He must go to Jerusalem and be killed.

- "From that time on, Jesus began to explain to His disciples that He must go to Jerusalem and suffer many things at the hands of the elders, chief priests and teachers of the law, and that He must be killed and on the third day be raised to life. Peter took Him aside and began to rebuke Him. 'Never, Lord,' he said. 'This shall never happen to you!' Jesus turned and said to Peter, 'Get behind me, Satan! You are a stumbling block to me; you do not have in mind the things of God, but the things of men.'" (Matthew 16:21-23)

Jesus' comment, "You do not have in mind the things of God but the things of men," plainly points out the problem of trying to interpret scripture without spiritual enlightenment. The scripture just seems to come alive when the Holy Spirit enables us to understand it. Without His guidance, we might even become a stumbling block to others by misinterpreting the scriptures or taking them out of context.

My hope is to share with you some of the pearls of truth which point to God's matchless glory and have led me to continually marvel at His grace and kindness.

One caveat here: The Holy Spirit makes His home in every Christian. So you or I may have come to understand a given scripture to a depth some others may not have reached. But it must also be the case that other Christians may display a fullness of understanding of certain scriptures for which you or I may have only a shallow knowledge. There is therefore no basis for pride or boasting by any of us in the matter of discovering the truth in God's Word.

CHAPTER 1

Discovering the Major Theme of the Bible

Take an exciting journey with me as we explore the scriptures which reveal and extol the major theme of the entire bible.

We must start with Paul's letter to the Ephesians and, as we go, include supporting scriptures from other books of the Bible.

Ephesians 1:3; 9-10; 11b: "Praise be to the God and Father of our Lord Jesus Christ, who has blessed us in the heavenly realms with every spiritual blessing in Christ. He made known to us the mystery of His will according to His good pleasure, which He purposed in Christ, to be put into effect when the times will have reached their fulfillment – *to bring unity to all things in heaven and on earth together under one Head, even*

Christ…predestined according to the plan of Him who works out everything in conformity with the purpose of His will." (*emphasis mine*)

In scripture the word 'mystery' as used in Ephesians and most other scriptures means something that is 'secret,' not something no one can understand. Please note what this mystery, or secret, is: *God intends to bring all things in heaven and on earth together (in peace) under Christ*, and furthermore, will work out everything in conformity with His will and at the time He intends.

Ephesians 1:22: "And God placed all things under His [Christ's] feet and appointed Him to be Head over everything for the church, which is His body, the fullness of Him who fills everything in every way."

Paul tells us that the fulfillment of the secret will involve the greatest act of humility recorded in the bible. First Corinthians 15:24-26, 28: "Then the end will come, when He [Christ] hands over the kingdom to God the Father after He has destroyed all dominion, authority and power. For He must reign until He has put all His enemies under His feet. The last enemy to be destroyed is death. When He has done this, then the Son Himself will be made subject to Him [God] who put everything under Him, so that God may be all in all!" The scope of the Son's act of submission to His Father at this point has no equal in the scriptures.

We are dealing with the account of One whom God exalted to the highest place, and gave a name above all other names (see Philippians 2:9-11) and at whose name every knee in the universe will bow and every tongue will confess Jesus Christ is Lord.

Jesus, the Messiah, God's Son, will make Himself subject to God His father so that He (God) may be all in all. (see 1 Corinthians 15:28) No act of humility by anyone else will ever come close to this.

Is it not clear that this mystery (*secret*), purposed by God to achieve permanent peace in the whole world (*all things in the heavens and on earth*) must be the dominant theme in all of Scripture? This mystery had been kept hidden in God for ages past. Being hidden in God means that God had not shared it with angels or men. It was hidden in the mind of God when He created the earth. It was hidden in God when the great flood wiped out all living creatures except those on the ark.

From the first to last page of scripture this mystery, now that it has been revealed, unveils God's intent for the world and His redemptive actions in Christ to accomplish His purpose to the end God may be all in all.

In Ephesians 3:21 Paul, in loving amazement at God's grand design exults: "to Him be glory in the Church and in Christ Jesus throughout all generations forever and ever! Amen!"

CHAPTER 2

The Church in God's Plan to Achieve Peace

But why should the church know this unless it is going to be involved in some way? And why is this revealed only in Paul's day? God intends to use the church in accomplishing His ultimate purpose! But Christ's church, though He spoke of it before His ascension to God's right hand, did not come into existence until Pentecost, at which time the Holy Spirit began His ministry of establishing the body of Christ as the church. There must be a head to direct its body. So it is imperative that the church, Christ's body, should be fully aware that God will use the church to eliminate the hostility between the Jew and the Gentile thus achieving peace among all the nations.

The nation Israel, at its inception, was assigned by God to display His glory to all the nations (Gentiles), and to facilitate their acceptance of the God of creation. Instead the Jews caused the Gentiles to blaspheme His name (see Romans 2:24). Hostility between Jew and Gentile was very evident even in Jesus' day. Jesus, in His first sermon at the synagogue in Nazareth, His home town, came close to being stoned because of His remarks about God sending Elijah to Zarephath to help a poor *Gentile* widow, bypassing many widows in Israel at that time. Jesus also reminded the synagogue that there were many with leprosy in Israel in Elisha's day, but only Naaman the *Syrian* was cleansed.

Let us then see how God planned to use the church to eliminate the hostility between Jews and Gentiles. Keep in mind that the rulers and authorities in the heavenly realms were well aware of this hostility and could not themselves fathom how God would achieve peace in the world, a peace that would draw all things in heaven and earth together under one head, Christ!

We know of course that when God unveiled His secret plan, hidden in Himself until the right time, it involved using the church to display His wisdom applied to achieving peace among all nations, Jew and Gentile, and in the process to destroy all the enemies of the Messiah.

Look then at Ephesians 2:14-18: "For He Himself is our peace, who has made the two [Jew and Gentile] one and has destroyed the barrier, the dividing wall of hostility, by abolishing in His flesh the law with its commandments and regulations. His purpose was to create *in Himself one new man out of the two*, thus making *peace*, and in this one body to reconcile both of them to God when He put to death their hostility. He came and preached *peace* to you who were far away [Gentiles] and *peace* to those who were near [Jews]. For through Him we both have access to the Father by one Spirit." (*emphasis mine*)

Note that the scripture does *not* say, "Create in Himself *one* man," but "one *new* man." What does that mean? That in the body of Christ, the Church, there is no longer Jew or Gentile. See Galatians 3:26-28: "You are all *sons of God* through faith in Christ Jesus, for all of you who are baptized into Christ have clothed yourselves with Christ. There is neither Jew nor Greek, slave nor free, male and female, for you are all one in Christ Jesus." (*emphasis mine*)

Be careful not to make the mistake of thinking Paul is talking about everyone in Christ being made equal. How can *one* be equal? But we are all *one* in Christ. So *equality* is not relevant, nor is it in view at all here. To speak of equality requires at least two of whatever

11

is being compared. Obviously Paul is not talking about each of us being equal to ourselves. Paul speaks of oneness, not equality. To further explain, look at 2 Corinthians 5:17-19, 21: "Therefore, if anyone is in Christ, he is a new creature [creation], the old has gone, the new has come! All this is from God, who reconciled us to Himself through Christ and gave us the ministry of reconciliation. That God was reconciling the world to Himself in Christ, not counting men's sins against them. God made Him who had no sin to be sin for us, so that in Him we might become the righteousness of God." He Himself is our peace!

In the church ethnicity is no longer relevant nor a source of hostility. The church body is neither Jew nor Gentile but *One New Man in Christ*. He, Christ, is our peace.

It should be no surprise that one of God's purposes for the church (see Ephesians 3:10) is to make known His manifold wisdom as discussed above. But to whom is this to be made known? It is now to be made known to the *rulers* and *authorities* in the heavenly realms. Ephesians 3:10: "His [God's] intent was that now, through the church, the manifold wisdom of God should be made known to the rulers and authorities in the heavenly realm." For some reason most of our commentators do not discuss Ephesians 3:10 when writing about the mission of the church. But when we understand that God's intent is to display His manifold wisdom to rulers and authorities through the church it helps us to see why it is critical that the church body must achieve and demonstrate the fullness of God.

Why does God want the rulers and authorities in the heavenly realm to understand His wisdom in using the church to achieve peace in all the nations? Until Christ's church became a reality, at Pentecost, it was not clear to them how God would eliminate hostility that had always existed between the Jew and the Gentile. Before the church, the rulers and authorities in the heavens could accuse God of being unable to establish peace in all the Gentile nations, both among themselves and, in particular, between Jews and Gentiles. God's enemies could say to Him, "Aha, God, you say you created man to manifest Your image and glory and rule the earth, but you started something you now cannot control. Look at all the fighting and vengeance on earth. We told you so! Have you forgotten you have already had to send a worldwide flood to wipe out all mankind, when, instead of peace, they filled the earth with violence?!"

With the creation of the 'one new man' in Christ, God's manifold wisdom in the process of achieving peace is revealed to the hostile forces of evil in the heavens, and His majesty and glory remain unassailable and has put to silence His critics.

Going back to Ephesians 1:9-10, Paul tells us: "For ages past the mystery of God's Will was kept hidden in God." To keep us on the same page, I repeat what this mystery is: *to bring all things in heaven and on earth together under one head, even Christ, and to accomplish this in accordance with His timing and good pleasure.*

The destruction of Christ's enemies must be accomplished in the process. Hostile enemies cannot be part of the "all things in Heaven and on Earth." Ephesians 1:20-23: Paul, in referring to God's mighty power for us who believe, tells us that "the power God exerted in raising Jesus from the dead was also used to seat Him [Jesus] at His right hand in the heavenly realms, far above all rule and authority, power and dominion, and every title that can be given, not only in the present age but also in the one to come. And God placed all things under His feet and appointed Him to be head over everything for the church, which is His body, the fullness of Him who fills everything in every way."

This amazing power is also spoken of by Paul in his first letter to the Corinthian church. See 1 Corinthians 15:24-26, 28: "Then the end will come, when He [Jesus] hands over the kingdom to God the Father

14

after He [Jesus] has destroyed all dominion, authority and power. *He must reign until He has put all His enemies under His feet.* The last enemy to be destroyed is death. When He has done this, then the Son Himself will be made subject to Him who put everything under Him, so that God may be all in all." (*emphasis mine*)

CHAPTER 3

About Satan and the Demonic Enemies of Jesus

Further study in Ephesians provides additional insight about the enemies of Christ. Ephesians 6:12: "For our struggle is not against flesh and blood, but against the rulers, against the authorities, against the world rulers of this darkness and against the spiritual forces of evil in the heavenly realms." These are all identified clearly and forcefully as the enemies of Christ which He will reduce to being nothing more than a footstool for His feet, after which He will present the kingdom devoid of enemies (even death) to His Father.

Many Christians, when they think of heaven, have in mind the picture of a place of perfect harmony and glorious peace, a place where God reigns and where nothing interferes with or challenges His majesty and omnipotence. If that were the case why would Jesus tell His disciples that He saw Satan fall like lightning from heaven? (Luke 10:18-20) And why would there be war in heaven? Revelations 12:3-4, 7-9: "Then another sign appeared in heaven: an enormous fiery red dragon with seven heads and ten horns and seven crowns [diadems] on his head. His tail swept a third of the stars out of the sky and flung them to the earth... And there was war in heaven. Michael and his angels fought against the dragon, and the dragon and his angels fought back. But he [the dragon] was not strong enough, and they lost their place [habitation] in heaven. The great dragon was hurled down—that ancient serpent called the devil, or Satan, who leads the whole world astray. He was hurled to the earth, and his angels with him." The first war ever was the one fought in heaven between Satan and his angels and Michael and his angels. Satan himself is referred to now as the ruler of the kingdom (domain) of the air. (see Ephesians 2:2)

All angels when created by God were good angels. Genesis 1:31: "God saw all that He had made, and it was very good."

It is clear that some of the angels did not remain obedient or continue to serve God as His angels of light. Satan, himself an angel, wanted to be equal to God. (see Isaiah 14:12-15 and Ezekiel 28:12-17) Denied this position, he became a slanderer and a blasphemer of God as evidenced by his temptation of Eve in Eden. In fact, Jesus, speaking of Satan to the Pharisees, said he was a murderer from the beginning. John 8:44: "You belong to your father, the devil, and you want to carry out your father's desire. He was a murderer from the beginning, not holding to the truth, for there is no truth in him. When he lies, he speaks his native language, for he is a liar and the father of lies." Deception is Satan's chief weapon in his warfare against God's people and all the nations as well.

Second Peter 2:4, 9 gives us additional insight: "For if God did not spare angels when they sinned, but sent them to Tartarus [the underworld, or abyss; used only here] putting them into gloomy dungeons [or chains of darkness] to be held for judgment—if this is so, then the Lord knows how to rescue godly men from trials and to hold the unrighteous for the day of judgment, while continuing their punishment."

Jude 6 says, "And the angels who did not keep their positions of authority but abandoned their own home [habitation]—these He has kept in *darkness*, bound with everlasting chains for judgment on the great day." They rejected 'light' so are kept in darkness.

Notice that the word 'darkness' is emphasized. Those angels who did not want to be angels of light had to relinquish their abode of light and would be kept in 'darkness' until the day of their final judgment.

All the evil spirits, or demons (angelic beings), knew precisely who Jesus was when, during His earthly ministry, He confronted them and ordered them to leave the bodies of those they had possessed. The angels who made up Satan's kingdom repeatedly referred to Jesus as the Son of God.

Matthew 8:28-29: "When He arrived at the other side in the region of the Gadarenes, two demon-possessed men coming from the tombs met Him. They were so violent that no one could pass that way. 'What do you want with us, Son of God?' they shouted! 'Have you come here to torment us before the appointed time?'"

Matthew 9:32,34: "While they were going out, a man who was demon-possessed and could not talk was brought to Jesus. And when the demon was driven out, the man who had been mute spoke...But the Pharisees said, 'It is by the prince of demons that He drives out demons.'"

Mark 5:6-8: "When he saw Jesus from a distance, he ran and fell on his knees in front of Him. He shouted at the top of his voice, 'What do you want with me, Jesus, Son of the Most High God? Swear to God that you won't torture me!' For Jesus had said to him, 'Come out of this man, you evil spirit!'"

Luke 4:3: "The devil said to Him, 'If you are the Son of God, tell this stone to become bread.'"

Luke 4:33-34: "In the synagogue there was a man possessed by a demon, an evil spirit. He cried out at the top of his voice, 'Ha! What do you want with us, Jesus of Nazareth? Have you come to destroy us? I know who you are—the Holy One of God!'"

Luke 4:41: "Moreover, many demons came out of many people, shouting, 'You are the Son of God!' But He rebuked them and would not allow them to speak, because they knew He was the Christ."

Those demons, or evil spirits, which were disobedient while God waited patiently in the days of Noah, are spoken of as spirits in prison. First Peter 3:18-20: "For Christ died for sins once for all, the righteous for the unrighteous, to bring you to God. He was put to death in the body but made alive by the Spirit, through whom also He went and preached to the spirits in prison who disobeyed long ago, when God waited patiently in the days of Noah while the ark was being built." Apparently only those angels disobedient in the days of Moses, not all disobedient angels, have been put in prison. Those Jesus Himself encountered during His earthly ministry were also disobedient, having left their 'home' and authority but obviously had not been imprisoned, yet they knew their time of judgment was coming.

So those in prison are not the demons which were possessing humans during the days of Christ on earth.

But even these demons knew their time was limited, and that they were condemned already. Listen to Matthew 8:29: "'What do you want with us, Son of God?' they shouted. 'Have you come here to torment us before the appointed time?'"

Mark 1:23-24: "Just then a man in their synagogue who was possessed by an evil spirit cried out, 'What do you want with us, Jesus of Nazareth? Have you come to destroy us? I know who you are—the Holy One of God!'"

It is noteworthy that, knowing God had appointed a time for their judgment and punishment, not one of these evil spirits is recorded as begging for forgiveness or for a second chance. God made no provision for forgiveness for an angel when it sinned. The Lord commanded angels not to speak nor even mention His name when He cast them out of the humans they were using as their 'home.' How would you feel if you had been ordered never to mention the name of Jesus and knew your sins would never be forgiven?

CHAPTER 4

The Shedding of Blood Prohibited

Genesis 9:5-7: "And for your lifeblood I will surely demand an accounting. I will demand an accounting from every animal. And from each man, too, I will demand an accounting for the life of his fellow man (or brother). Whoever sheds the blood of man, by man shall his blood be shed, for in the image of God has God made man. As for you, be fruitful and increase in number, multiply on the earth and increase upon it."

Please note that God established civil government as one means of curbing the revengeful shedding of man's blood, so widespread it led to a worldwide flood. This prohibition is not recorded until the ninth chapter of Genesis, after the flood had destroyed every living creature on earth except those in the ark.

The following scripture describes what God saw when He looked at the condition of humankind before the flood.

Genesis 6:11-13, 17: "Now the earth was corrupt in God's sight and was full of violence. God saw how corrupt the earth had become, for all the people on earth had corrupted their ways. So God said to Noah, 'I am going to put an end to all people, for the earth is filled with violence because of them. I am surely going to destroy both them *and the earth*...I am going to bring floodwaters on the earth to destroy all life under the heavens, every creature that has the breath of life in it. Everything on earth will perish.'" (*emphasis mine*)

The genealogy of Cain makes a point of describing the technologies developed by his descendants and the failure of their inventions to curb vengeance and violence. It also points to the first reference to polygamy. (see Genesis 4:17-24) Technology, of itself, does not ensure morality.

There is a somewhat humorous wordplay here. In the Hebrew language the land outside Eden is referred to as the land of Nod. A wanderer is a Nad. So Cain complains *He will just be a Nad in Nod.*

"Cain lay with his wife and she became pregnant and gave birth to Enoch. Cain was then building a city, and he named it after his son Enoch. To Enoch was born Irad, and Irad was the father of Mehujael, and Mehujael was the father of Methushael, and Methushael was the father of Lamech. Lamech married two women, one named Adah and the other Zillah. Adah gave birth to Jabel; he was the father of those who live in tents and raise livestock. His brother's name was Jubal; he was the father of all who play the harp and flute. Zillah also had a son, Tubal-Cain, who forged all kinds of tools out of bronze and iron. Tubal-Cain's sister was Naamah. Lamech said to his wives, 'Adah and Zillah, listen to me; wives of Lamech, hear my words; I have killed a man for wounding me, a young man for injuring me. If Cain is avenged seven times, then Lamech seventy-seven times.'" (Genesis 4:17-24)

We should understand that following Cain's murder of his brother Abel, God did not cut off Cain but marked him so no one would try to kill him to avenge Abel's death. God stated that whoever killed Cain would suffer vengeance seven times over. So God left Cain alive to make His point!

Genesis 4:13: "Cain said to the Lord, 'My punishment is more than I can bear. Today you are driving me from the land and I will be hidden from your presence; I will be a restless wanderer on the earth, and whoever finds me will kill me.' But the Lord said to him, 'Not so; if anyone kills Cain, he will suffer vengeance seven times over.'"

As noted above, Lamech boasted to his two wives about killing a man who had wounded him saying, "If Cain is avenged seven times, then Lamech seventy-seven times." This points to a major reason why the earth was filled with violence at that time – the thirst of man for individual revenge, leading to the shedding of human blood by any individual seeking revenge whenever a relative or friend had been killed, even accidentally.

But someone might say, "Why is Seth's genealogy interposed at this point? How does it contribute to vengeance and violence? Why is it included in the lead up to the flood?" It occupies the entire fifth chapter and the last two verses of chapter six. Genesis 4:25-26: "Adam lay with his wife again, and she gave birth to a son and named him Seth, saying, 'God has granted me another child in place of Abel, since Cain killed him.' Seth also had a son, and he named him Enosh. At that time, men began to call on the name of the Lord."

There is a deliberate contrast in Seth's line, which produced Enoch who walked with God 300 years, with the polygamist and murderer Lamech, of Cain's line, who walked after his own way and thumbed his nose at God's prohibition of violence and vengeance. (see Genesis 4:23-24)

"Lamech said to his wives, Adah and Zillah, 'Listen to me; wives of Lamech, hear my words. I have killed a man for wounding me, a young man for injuring me. If Cain is avenged seven times, then Lamech seventy-seven times.'" However, nothing is said in Seth's genealogy about anyone seeking revenge by or against anyone.

Seth's genealogy can be traced through Noah all the way to Terah, the father of Abram, as recorded in Genesis 11:27. But we should also notice something that is a constant refrain throughout this extended genealogy. The phrase "and had other sons and daughters" is first noted in Genesis 5:3-4 with regard to Adam. After Seth was born, Adam lived 800 years "and had other sons and daughters." We are never given the names of these sons and daughters. This refrain is attached to each of the named men in Seth's genealogy except Noah.

What is being recorded then is a select genealogy. It was selected, or chosen, by God to take us all the way from Adam to Abram with whom God made a covenant to establish a nation for His own inheritance, the nation of Israel.

What we must not forget is that all these men in the select genealogy had other children, male and female who, along with the progeny of Ham and Japheth, Noah's other sons, must have accounted for the entire human race in their day. This is emphasized in Genesis 9:18a, 19: "The sons of Noah who came out of the ark were Shem, Ham and Japheth...These were the three sons of Noah, and from them came the people who were scattered over the earth."

Genesis 10:5 sums up the progeny of Japheth this way: "From these the maritime peoples spread out into their territories by their clans within their nations, each with its own language."

Of Ham it is recorded: "These are the sons of Ham by their clans and languages, in their territories and nations." Summarizing, Genesis 10:32 states: "These are the clans of Noah's sons, according to their lines of descent, within the nations. From these the nations spread out over the earth after the flood." This took place after God confused their language so they would not be able to work together in harmony, forcing them against their will to disperse into all the earth. (see Genesis 11:8-9)

Returning to Genesis 6:5-7, "The Lord saw how great man's wickedness on the earth had become, and that every inclination of the thoughts of his heart was only evil all the time. The Lord was grieved that He had made man on the earth, and His heart was filled with pain. So the Lord said, 'I will wipe mankind, whom I have created, from the face of the earth—men and animals, and creatures that move along the ground, and birds of the air—for I am grieved that I have made them.'"

Genesis 6:11-13: "Now the earth was corrupt in God's sight and was full of violence. God saw how corrupt the earth had become, for all the people on earth had corrupted their ways. So God said to Noah, 'I am going to put an end to all people, for the earth is filled with violence because of them. I am surely going to destroy both them and the earth.'"

During this account of the flood and the ark, the scripture emphasizes how extensive this flood was. Genesis 7:18-20: "The waters rose and increased greatly on the earth, and the ark floated on the surface of the water. They rose greatly on the earth, and *all the high mountains under the entire heavens were covered*. The waters rose and covered the mountains to a depth of more than twenty feet." (*emphasis mine*)

Many Christians seem to have trouble believing the flood was global. But if you are in this group you must decide whether you are going to believe the scripture just cited or not. The scripture states plainly that all the mountains under the *entire* heavens were covered. Taken at face value no room is left for thinking the flood was only local.

In addition to establishing civil government to render justice when blood is shed, instead of allowing unfettered vengeance by individuals, God also established *covenant* relationships with mankind throughout the Bible. The first mention of this word is found in Genesis 6:18: "But I will establish my covenant with you, and you will enter the ark—you and your sons and your wife and your sons' wives with you."

After the flood waters had receded, Noah's family and all the animals left the ark and Noah built an altar on which he sacrificed some of the animals. Then God elaborated on His covenant with Noah, saying in His heart, "Never again will I curse the ground because of man, even though every inclination of his heart is evil from childhood. And never again will I destroy all living creatures as I have done. As long as the earth endures, seedtime and harvest, cold and heat, summer and winter, day and night will never cease." (see Genesis 8:18-22)

Think about the context in which God made His covenant with Noah. God blessed Noah and his sons, telling them, "Be fruitful and increase in number and fill the earth." (Genesis 9:1) Notice that, in Genesis 1, when God brought Eve to Adam to be his wife, He said to them, "Be fruitful and increase in number; fill the earth and *subdue* it. *Rule* over the fish of the sea and the birds of the air and over ever living creature that moves on the ground." (Genesis 1:28) In Genesis 1:26 God said, "Let us make man in our image, in our likeness, and let them...*rule over all the earth*." (*emphasis mine*)

But in Genesis 9:1 nothing is said about ruling over the earth. It appears that Adam and Eve, by agreeing with Satan's slander and blasphemy of God in the garden, and by agreeing to do as Satan suggested (eating from the tree forbidden to them) handed over to Satan their mandate to rule over the earth and subdue it! When Satan tempted Jesus in the wilderness, "He took Him up to a high place and showed Him in an instant all the kingdoms of the world and he said to Him, 'I will give you all their authority and splendor, for *it has been given to me*, and I can give it to anyone I want to. So if you worship me, it will all be yours.' Jesus answered, 'It is written, worship the Lord your God and serve Him only.'" (Luke 4:5-8, *emphasis mine*) Jesus gave no indication Satan could not do as he said. The Lord's reply to Satan was precisely what Adam and Eve should have said to him, "Worship the Lord your God and serve Him only!"

Returning to Genesis, God told Noah that He was giving, in addition to the green plants, "everything that lives and moves as food for you." (Genesis 9:3)

However, eating meat with its lifeblood still in it was prohibited, as also the shedding of blood of man by man or animal. Genesis 9:5-6: "And for your lifeblood I will surely demand an accounting. I will demand an accounting from every animal. And from each man, too, I will demand an accounting for the life of his fellow man [brother]. Whoever sheds the blood of man, by man shall his blood be shed; for in the image of God has God made man."

This scripture about shedding the blood of man refers back to what God was speaking about in Genesis 6:11-12: "Now the earth was corrupt in God's sight and was full of violence. God saw how corrupt the earth had become, for all the people on earth had corrupted their ways." This has to be a reference to violent, vindictive murder by individual persons in pursuit of revenge. Nothing less than this would result in an earth full of violence.

Curbing intentional murder in the service of justice requires a civil government acting as God's agent, or as in the case later on, a nation under a covenant of law, devoted to the display of God as creator of the universe. A disinterested party, acting in God's behalf, must determine if the shedding of blood was deliberate or unintentional. Later on, to emphasize this requirement, God had the nation of Israel set aside six of its cities as cities of refuge to which anyone involved in bloodshed could go until an investigation was completed. These cities were located throughout Israel so that anyone would be able to reach one or the other in one day. The roads to these cities were to be kept in perfect condition with no impediments to anyone involved in shedding human blood trying to reach the nearest city before an avenger could intercept him.

However, look at Genesis 9:7: "As for you, be fruitful and increase in number; multiply on the earth and increase upon it." Why is this verse located here; seemingly not related to the context? Verse 7 is a repetition of verse 3. So in this setting its most probable purpose is to link abortion to the prohibition of shedding blood. *Abortion flies in the face of being fruitful, increasing in number* and filling the earth. Abortion is the shedding not only of innocent blood but the shedding of *defenseless* innocent blood, the worst form of intentional murder.

To facilitate the safety and growth of an unborn infant God provided a 'safe house' for the baby's first nine months of life – the mother's womb. Performing an abortion requires that the safe house be invaded and its occupant dismembered and removed part by part.

This is a ghastly, gruesome procedure by any measure. A mother who authorizes the murder of her baby as described, if unrepentant, will from that time on, for the rest of her life, forfeit a clear conscience.

In our culture today, when authorizing an abortion, the father is never mentioned, and of the mother it is said, in defense of justifying such a hideous murder, "A woman has a right to do with her body as she chooses," meaning that if she decides to have her baby aborted she has a right to do so. This senseless mantra completely overlooks the fact that the baby is NOT her body. If it were, when the baby is killed, her own body would die also. Nor is it true that anyone, male or female, has a right to do with their own body whatever they please. We have the right and obligation to do what pleases God. (see Ephesians 5:10)

God holds both father and mother responsible for the life of their baby. She must nourish and cherish it into childhood. Fathers have overall responsibility for the upbringing of sons and daughters in the ways of God. (see Ephesians 6:4) In Deuteronomy the father is admonished seven times by God through Moses to have the commandments of God on their minds. See Deuteronomy 6:4-7: "Hear, O Israel: The Lord our God, the Lord is one. Love the Lord your God with all your heart and with all your soul and with all your strength. These commandments that I give you today are to be upon your hearts. Impress them on your children. Talk about them when you sit at home and when you walk along the road, when you lie down and when you get up." Deuteronomy 7:6: "For you are a people holy to the Lord your God. The Lord your God has chosen you out of all the peoples on the face of the earth to be His people, His treasured possession."

In the New Testament Paul also discusses God's prohibition against individual revenge. Romans 12:17-13:1: "Do not repay anyone evil for evil. Be careful to do what is right in the eyes of everybody. If it is possible, as far as it depends on you, live at peace with everyone. Do not take revenge, my friends, but leave room for God's wrath, for it is written: 'it is mine to avenge; I will repay,' says the Lord. On the contrary: 'If your enemy is hungry, feed him; if he is thirsty, give him something to drink. In doing this, you will heap burning coals on his head.' Do not be overcome by evil, but overcome evil with good. Everyone must submit himself to the governing authorities, for there is no authority except that which God has established. The authorities that exist have been established by God."

A clear understanding of the early chapters of Genesis makes it plain that God imposes serious responsibilities on government authorities in the care of their people. The first duty of any government is to protect the safety of its people. It must regulate bloodshed. Every government has the duty of imposing capital punishment on intentional murder, of which abortion is the parade example. Putting intentional murderers in prison for life instead of imposing the death sentence is a travesty of justice and displays a government that refuses to listen to God's directive or act as His agent in the matter. In the case of our own country, the refusal of capital punishment has resulted in unserved justice, overcrowded prisons, and undue burdens on tax payers.

The government that disobeys God's injunction cannot endure. Such governments spit in God's face when they refuse to administer capital punishment on a timely basis. The characteristics of a government functioning as God intends are: 1) execution of Justice and 2) the display of Righteousness.

Isaiah 1:21: "See how the faithful city has become a harlot! She once was full of justice; righteousness used to dwell in her – but now murderers!"

Isaiah 9:7b: "…He will reign on David's throne and over his kingdom, establishing and upholding it with justice and righteousness from that time on and forever…"

Isaiah 11:4: "...but with righteousness He will judge the needy, with justice He will give decisions for the poor of the earth."

Isaiah 16:5: "In love a throne will be established; in faithfulness a man will sit on it – one from the house of David – one who in judging seeks justice and speeds the cause of righteousness."

Isaiah 28:17: "I will make justice the measuring line and righteousness the plumb line…"

Isaiah 32:1: "See, a king will reign in righteousness and rulers will rule with justice."

Isaiah 32:16-17: "Justice will dwell in the desert and righteousness live in the fertile field."

Isaiah 33:5: "The Lord is exalted, for He dwells on high; He will fill Zion with justice and righteousness."

Enough said?

CHAPTER 5

God's Covenant With Noah and Every Living Creature

Genesis 9:8-11: "Then God said to Noah and to his sons with him, 'I now establish my covenant with you and with your descendants after you and with every living creature that was with you – the birds, the livestock and all the wild animals, all those who came out of the ark with you – every living creature on earth. I establish my covenant with you: never again will all life be cut off by the waters of a flood, never again will there be a flood to destroy the earth.'"

Genesis 9:12-17: "And God said, 'This is the sign of the covenant I am making between me and you and every living creature with you, a covenant for all generations to come. I have set my rainbow in the clouds, and it will be the sign of the covenant between me and the earth. Whenever I bring clouds over the earth and the rainbow appears in the clouds, I will remember my covenant between me and you and all living creatures of every kind. Never again will the waters become a flood to destroy all life. Whenever the rainbow appears in the clouds, I will see it and remember the everlasting covenant between God and all living creatures of every kind on the earth.' So God said to Noah, 'This is the sign of the covenant I have established between me and all life on the earth.'"

This covenant was between God and every living creature on earth. It is said to be a covenant for all generations to come and is called an everlasting covenant. God told Noah that when the sign of the covenant, the rainbow in the clouds appears, He will see it and remember the everlasting covenant between God and all living creatures of every kind on the earth.

This covenant was also unilateral; the institution or continued existence of the covenant did not depend on man doing – or not doing – anything. It existed solely by the promise of God and applied to all living things at all times. Jesus Himself referred to this covenant when He said, "Love your enemies and pray for those who persecute you, that you may be sons of your Father in heaven. He causes His sun to rise on the evil and the good, and sends rain on the righteous and the unrighteous." (Matthew 5:44-45)

God's covenant proves there is no such thing as 'evolution.' There is nothing random about His covenant. God reiterated to Noah that as long as the earth endures it would function in accordance with established predictable laws: seedtime and harvest, cold and heat, summer and winter, day and night will never cease. How can such certitude exist along with the random nature of evolution which is dependent upon unpredictable change, the outcome of which is anything but certain? Not one sentence says anything about something evolving. The sun will rise tomorrow in the morning because God says it will, not because of evolution. There is no evidence today anywhere of anything 'evolving.'

This is the promise God made in His covenant: 1) Never again will all life be cut off by the waters of a flood. 2) Never again will there be a flood to destroy the earth. 3) Never again will the waters become a flood to destroy all life. Please note the repetition of God's promise. Three times God assures Noah neither the earth nor any life on it will ever again be destroyed by water.

The extent of the destruction caused by the worldwide flood included the destruction of the *earth*. The ground is specifically mentioned. In Genesis 8:21b, the Lord said: "Never again will I curse the ground because of man." This refers back to Genesis 3:17a:

"To Adam He said, 'Because you listened to your wife and ate from the tree about which I commanded you, You must not eat of it, cursed is the ground because of you.'"

This curse ceased to be relevant when God destroyed the earth in the flood. The surface of the earth was greatly changed. After the flood there were valleys where none had been, new mountains, and rivers and seas in different places. God said to Noah He would never *again* curse the ground. The curse was that the ground would produce thorns and thistles requiring Adam great effort to produce food. If the ground had remained under the curse of God after the flood, the word 'again' would not have been used in His promise to Noah. Just as God told Noah that never again will all life be cut off by the waters of a flood (Genesis 9:11), 'again' must be taken to show there will no longer be any curse on the ground because of man. (Genesis 8:21)

God's covenant with all life on earth is still in force today and will remain in force even after God makes a new heaven and new earth. Revelation 21:1: "Then I saw a new heaven and a new earth, for the first heaven and the first earth had passed away, and there was no longer any sea." That God never intends ever again to use water to destroy the earth, including the new earth, seems quite clear.

There is a rather humorous incident recorded in Revelation 12:13-16 regarding an attempt by Satan to use water to destroy the woman who gave birth to the One who would rule all the nations. She is representative of the nation of Israel. Satan is not only the deceiver of all the nations but is also a copycat. "When the dragon saw that he had been hurled to the earth, he pursued the woman who had given birth to the male child. The woman was given the two wings of a great eagle, so that she might fly to the place prepared for her in the desert, where she would be taken care of for a time, times and half a time, out of the serpent's reach. Then from his mouth the serpent spewed water like a river, to overtake the woman and sweep her away with the torrent. But the earth helped the woman by opening its mouth and swallowing the river that the dragon had spewed out of his mouth."

Guess where Satan probably got the idea of using water to destroy the woman? It seems obvious he was trying to use water as a destructive force just as he saw God use the water of a global flood to destroy the earth and mankind.

But whereas it was *words* coming from Satan's *mouth* in the garden with Eve that accomplished his purpose then, so now in Revelation, it is his intent by a torrential river of *water* from his *mouth* to thwart the woman's safety and show God a thing or two! It did not occur to Satan that the earth itself would open *its mouth* and swallow up the river he spewed forth. This was the opposite of what the earth did in producing rain for forty days and nights, as described in Genesis 7:11. "In the six-hundredth year of Noah's life, on the seventeenth day of the second month – on that day all the springs of the great deep burst, and the floodgates of the heavens were opened." At that time the earth opened its mouth, in conjunction with the gates of the heavens opening up, to deluge the world with water from above and below from the great deep.

Satan's rejoinder however is anything but humorous. Revelation 12:17: "Then the dragon was enraged at the woman and went off to make war against the rest of her offspring – those who obey God's commandments and hold to the testimony of Jesus."

CHAPTER 6

Elijah and Elisha

One of the most unusual pearls of truth in scripture is found in 1 Kings 16:29 through 2 Kings 13:21. This section of scripture relates to the time after the twelve tribes of Israel (the nation of Israel) had left Egypt and settled in the promised land. Each tribe had been assigned a specific territory. Later, in response to a very insensitive king (one of Solomon's sons) they split into a northern kingdom, lasting from 931 to 722 BC, comprised of all the tribes with their land except the tribes of Judah and Benjamin, and a southern kingdom comprised of only the tribes of Judah and Benjamin (to be understood as part of the southern kingdom when the house of Judah is mentioned).

During the time of the two kingdoms, the northern kingdom was referred to as the house of Israel and the southern kingdom as the house of Judah. In the northern kingdom Jeroboam, their first king, had two golden calves made, one placed at Bethel, only a few miles north of Jerusalem, and the other calf placed in the northern part of the kingdom, in the tribe of Dan's territory. These locations were chosen to discourage the tribes living in the northern kingdom from continuing to go to Jerusalem to the temple to present their sacrifices and offerings to God. Their king reasoned that if the people continued to go to Jerusalem to worship, he would sooner or later be ousted as their king and thus lose the kingdom. He arbitrarily chose men to be priests at the altar in Bethel who were not from the tribe of Levi and thus not acceptable for service at God's altar.

During the northern kingdom's existence, not one of their twenty kings was godly. During Elisha's ministry, he anointed Jehu, son of Nimshi, the best of the lot, to be king of the northern kingdom. Jehu established a dynasty in which four generations of his progeny occupied the throne.

Elijah began his ministry while Ahab was king. Jehu, as directed by God through Elisha, was responsible for the death of all of Ahab's sons and descendants. More about Jehu later.

We concentrate now on two of God's most notable Old Testament prophets, Elijah and then at his death, Elisha. These two prophets were commissioned by God to prophesy to the northern kingdom during the time when Baal worship was established as the state religion and promoted by Jezebel, one of Ahab's wives.

The ministries of these two men are remarkable. They were not writing prophets like Isaiah or one of the minor prophets. Elijah is introduced to us in 1 Kings 17:1-4: "Now Elijah the Tishbite, from Tishbe in Gilead, said to Ahab, 'As the Lord, the God of Israel, lives, whom I serve, there will be neither dew nor rain in the next few years except at my word.'" We do not get the significance of what Elijah said until we turn back to 1 Kings 16:29-33: "In the thirty-eighth year of Asa king of Judah, Ahab son of Omri became king of Israel, and he reigned in Samaria over Israel twenty-two years. Ahab son of Omri did more evil in the eyes of the Lord than any of those before him. He not only considered it trivial to commit the sins of Jeroboam son of Nebat, but he also married Jezebel, daughter of Ethbaal, king of the Sidonians, and began to serve Baal and worship him. He set up an altar for Baal in the temple of Baal that he built in Samaria. Ahab also made an Asherah pole and did more to provoke the Lord, the God of Israel to anger than did all the kings of Israel before him."

Ahab, under the influence of Jezebel, made Baal worship the state religion of the house of Israel. This could not have been more contrary to God's plans for the nation He had chosen for Himself and through which He intended to proclaim His sovereignty and almighty power to all the other nations in the world. "If you ever forget the Lord your God and follow other gods and worship and bow down to them, I testify against you today that you will surely be destroyed. Like the nations the Lord destroyed before you, so you will be destroyed for not obeying the Lord your God." (Deuteronomy 8:19-20) "So if you faithfully obey the commands I am giving you today – to love the Lord your God and to serve Him with all your heart and with all your soul – then I will send *rain* on your land in its season, both autumn and spring rains, so that you may gather in your grain, new wine and oil. I will provide grass in the fields for your cattle, and you will eat and be satisfied. Be careful or you will be enticed to turn away and worship other gods and bow down to them. Then the Lord's anger will burn against you, and He will shut the heavens so that it will not rain and the ground will yield no produce, and you will soon perish from the good land the Lord is giving you." (Deuteronomy 11:16-17)

Returning to Elijah's first recorded meeting with Ahab (see 1 Kings 17:1) it is obvious he is not just passing the time of day or making a few comments on the weather to the king. He comes straight to the point. "It ain't gonna rain until I say so." This is a direct reprimand of Ahab and puts him on notice that not all the Baals in the land will be able to cause it to rain.

A word or two about Baal is in order. Baal, whether of a specific town, place or family, was thought to be the storm god and god of fertility. The Baals were therefore believed to give the rain in season by setting off storms across the land. So Elijah is confirming to Ahab that he is in open rebellion to the God of Israel and is leading the northern kingdom to trust and worship the Baals, precisely what God had forbidden.

Of course the lack of rain caused a famine in the land. How long did this famine last? We know the answer because we are told in the New Testament how long it was. "I assure you that there were many widows in Israel in Elijah's time, when the sky was shut for three and a half years and there was a severe famine throughout the land." (Luke 4:25) "Elijah was a man just like us. He prayed earnestly that it would not rain, and it did not rain on the land for three and a half years. Again he prayed, and the heavens gave rain, and the earth produced its crops." (James 5:17-18)

As we would suspect, Elijah became Ahab's enemy. God directed Elijah to hide from Ahab in the Kerith Ravine, east of the Jordan River and was directed by God to get water from the brook at that place. God sent ravens to bring food to Elijah twice a day. Ravens were unclean according to Leviticus 11:15, but God chose ravens to scavenge and bring bread and meat to Elijah. Normally anything touching someone or something unclean would itself be considered unclean.

This seems to be a case where the circumstances and common sense override any law about ceremonial uncleanness. Consider an incident in the New Testament involving Jesus and working on the Sabbath to illustrate the point. "Indignant because Jesus had healed on the Sabbath, the synagogue ruler said to the people, 'There are six days for work. So come and be healed on those days, not on the Sabbath.' The Lord answered him, 'You hypocrites! Doesn't each of you on the Sabbath untie his ox or donkey from the stall and lead it out to give it water? Then should not this woman, a daughter of Abraham, whom Satan has kept bound for eighteen long years, be set free on the Sabbath day from what bound her?' When he had said this, all his opponents were humiliated, but the people were delighted with all the wonderful things he was doing." (Luke 13:14-17)

I'm sure the ravens also showed up on the Sabbath, aren't you?

Finally the water in the brook dried up. God instructed Elijah to go to Zarephath and stay there with a widow who would provide food and water for him. Would you not agree with me that God's ways are not man's ways? First a raven, then a poor gentile widow, were ordered to feed Elijah.

To get to Zarephath, Elijah had to go across the land from east of the Jordan River to the coast of the Mediterranean Sea to a suburb of Sidon, and to do this at the very time Ahab's troops were on an all out hunt for him. During all the time Elijah was in hiding in the Kerith Ravine, Ahab had special forces out looking for him, and Ahab's wife, Jezebel, was seeking out the other prophets of God to put them to death (see 2 Kings 9:7).

When God sent Elijah to Zarephath, He was in effect sending him into the lion's den. Zarephath was a suburb of both Tyre and Sidon, the very center of Baal worship. Jezebel's father was the king of Sidon and chief priest of Baalism. The last place Ahab would think to search for Elijah would be in the heart of Baal territory, his back yard so to speak. How astonishing and exciting it is to see what God does and how God does it.

But God did not send Elijah just for his own sake to Zarephath. He was sent there so a poor widow would know the truth about the God of Israel. She had been questioning in her heart what was being taught about Baal and also what she had heard about the God of Israel. In other words she wanted to know the truth. This put her in a special category. It is a blessed category because God will respond to anyone who wants to know the truth about God. That is as true today as it was then.

Let us look closely at Elijah's first meeting with the widow. "So he went to Zarephath. When he came to the town gate, a widow was there gathering sticks. He called to her and asked, 'Would you bring me a little water in a jar so I may have a drink?' As she was going to get it, he called, 'and bring me, please, a piece of bread.'" (1 Kings 17:10-11) Bear in mind God had not given Elijah the name of the widow. In fact, nowhere in this account is the name of the widow given. For starters how would he know the woman picking up sticks (wood) was a widow? I think that her activity when he first saw her at the town gate indicated she had no husband. Normally a husband would be gathering wood, not his wife. An example of a man gathering wood is found in Numbers 15:32.

How would Elijah identify this particular widow as the one God had ordered to feed him when he got to Zarephath? By asking any widow he met on arrival for water and food. In a town of any size there would likely be more than one widow. Had she simply refused a request for food he would have known she was not the widow whom God had ordered to feed him. "As surely as the Lord your God lives," she replied, "I don't have any bread – only a handful of flour in a jar and a little oil in a jug. I am gathering a few sticks to take home and make a meal for myself and my son, that we may eat it – and die." Given what she said to Elijah about her lack of food further indicated that she was indeed a widow and would not be likely to prepare the last of her food for some man she had never seen before unless she was indeed the widow God had told him about. "Elijah said to her, 'Don't be afraid. Go home and do as you have said. But *first* make a small cake of bread for me from what you have and bring it to me, and then make something for yourself and your son. For this is what the Lord, the God of Israel says, 'The jar of flour will not be used up and the jug of oil will not run dry until the day the Lord gives rain on the land.' She went away and did as Elijah had told her. So there was food every day for Elijah and for the woman and her family. For the jar of flour was not used up and the jug of oil did not run dry, [this verifying to her that he was a man of God] in keeping with the word of the Lord spoken by Elijah." (1 Kings 17:12-16)

In this way Elijah recognized the widow to whom he had been sent and the widow realized Elijah was a prophet of the God of Israel, and the one she should feed. Remember her statement – "As surely as the *Lord your God* lives" – indicating not only that she knew about the God of Israel but she also must have assumed at this point that Elijah was a man come from God. Had he been a prophet of Baal he would have set her straight soon enough. Perhaps God had given her a heads-up that someone would be sent to her to help her find out about this God of Israel.

Some time later the widow's son died. Her anguished remark to Elijah gives us more insight into her thinking. "She said to Elijah, 'What do you have against me, man of God? Did you come to remind me of my sin and kill my son?' Elijah carried the boy to his upper room and said to God, 'O Lord my God, have you brought tragedy also upon this widow I am staying with by causing her son to die?' Then he stretched himself out on the boy three times and cried to the Lord, 'O Lord my God, let this boy's life return to him!' The Lord heard Elijah's cry, and the boy's life returned to him. Elijah returned the widow's son to her. Then the woman said to Elijah, 'Now I know that you are a man of God and that the word of the Lord from your mouth is the truth!'" (1 Kings 17:17-24)

From this unusual account of Elijah and the widow we can assert that she had been looking for the truth as to whom she should depend on in her need and was apparently unsatisfied with what was commonly believed about Baalism. Nowhere in the scriptures is anything said about Baal urging any of his followers to provide assistance to widows in need – or to anyone in need for that matter. Those who worshipped

Baal were not encouraged to love and care for one another. Of all the things people believed about Baal, raising the dead to life was not one of them. Actually, it was taught about Baal that he himself died after the rainy season and had to be resurrected each year all over again.

God holds in high regard those who seek the truth about Him. This account shows God sending His premier prophet through enemy territory, where he was being sought day and night by Ahab's soldiers, to a widow of no repute who had been seeking the truth day and night. Her last words say it all: *"Now I know."* Is this not the kind of God you and I need? One who loves us unfailingly despite our sin? It was not Baal who died on our behalf but Jesus, the Son of God.

Much later, in the third year of the famine, Elijah sought out Obadiah, who was in charge of Ahab's palace, and told him to notify Ahab where he was. Obadiah was very fearful about telling Ahab he knew where Elijah was, a feat none of Ahab's army had been able to accomplish. Obadiah related to Elijah how extensive their search had been and that he had hidden many of God's prophets in caves to protect them from Jezebel's vengeful hand. "As surely as the Lord your God lives, there is not a nation or kingdom where my master has not sent someone to look for you. And whenever a nation or kingdom claimed you were not there, he made them swear they could not find you. But now you tell me to go to my master and say, 'Elijah is here.'" (1 Kings 18:10-11) Although very fearful Obadiah did as Elijah directed.

So Ahab met Elijah and accused him of being the troubler of Israel. "After a long time, in the third year, the word of the Lord came to Elijah 'Go and present yourself to Ahab, and I will send rain on the land.' So Elijah went to present himself to Ahab. Now the famine was severe in Samaria, and Ahab had summoned Obadiah, who was in charge of his palace. (Obadiah was a devout believer in the Lord. While Jezebel was killing off the Lord's prophets, Obadiah had taken a hundred prophets and hidden them in two caves, fifty in each, and had supplied them with food and water.) Ahab had said to Obadiah, 'Go through the land to all the springs and valleys. Maybe we can find some grass to keep the horses and mules alive so we will not have to kill any of our animals.' So they divided the land they were to cover, Ahab going in one direction and Obadiah in another." (1 Kings 18:1-6)

Note that Ahab's concern was not about Jezebel killing the prophets of God but about possibly having to kill his animals. What are we to think about such a man? It is not possible that Ahab was unaware of his wife's hatred for God's prophets. Whether he cared or not, God's word about the proper treatment of prophets, His or false prophets, or prophets of man-made gods, is clear. Let's review God's directives in the matter.

Deuteronomy 13:1-5: "If a prophet, or one who foretells by dreams, appears among you and announces to you a miraculous sign or wonder, and if the sign or wonder of which he has spoken takes place, and he says, 'Let us follow other gods (gods you have not known) and let us worship them,' you must not listen to the words of that prophet or dreamer. The Lord your God is testing you to find out whether you love Him with all your heart and with all your soul. It is the Lord your God you must follow, and Him you must revere. Keep His commands and obey Him; serve Him and hold fast to Him. That prophet or dreamer must be put to death, because he preached rebellion against the Lord your God, who brought you out of Egypt and redeemed you from the land of slavery; he has tried to turn you away from the way the Lord your God commanded you to follow. You must purge the evil from among you." Deuteronomy 18:15: "The Lord your God will raise up for you a prophet like me from among your brothers. You must listen to him."

It will be profitable for us to fast forward to the meeting of Jesus with Moses and Elijah on the Mount of Transfiguration and listen to God's command to Peter, James and John who were also there. This is the occasion when Jesus, just the week before, had informed the disciples that He must be put to death at Jerusalem. The disciples rejected this announcement to put it mildly.

This is what happened on the Mount. Matthew 17:4-5: "Peter said to Jesus, 'Lord it is good for us to be here. If You wish, I will put up three shelters – one for you, one for Moses and one for Elijah.' While he was still speaking, a bright cloud enveloped them, and a voice from the cloud said, 'This is my Son, whom I love; with Him I am well pleased. Listen to Him!'" On other occasions God spoke audibly from heaven about Jesus. (His announcement to John in Mark 1:9-11 identifying Jesus as the Messiah is a good example.) But only on the Mount of Transfiguration does God say, "Listen to Him." We need to understand in our day we cannot improve on this directive. While Peter was offering to build shelters for Jesus, Moses and Elijah, God was saying. "Listen to Jesus, not Peter nor anyone else." The disciples heard Moses and Elijah talking to Jesus about His upcoming crucifixion and ascension.

Back to Deuteronomy 18:20: "But a prophet who presumes to speak in my name anything I have not commanded him to say, or a prophet who speaks in the name of other gods, must be put to death."

Deuteronomy 18:21-22: "You may say to yourselves, 'How can we know when a message has not been spoken by the Lord?' If what a prophet proclaims in the name of the Lord does not take place or come true, that is a message the Lord has not spoken. That prophet has spoken presumptuously. Do not be afraid of him."

This review of the status of a prophet, or anyone claiming to be a prophet or to speak in God's name, is pertinent at this point in Elijah's ministry. At his second meeting with Ahab, during the third year of the famine he had announced to Ahab at their first meeting, he told Ahab, "…You have abandoned the Lord's commands and have followed the Baals. Now summon the people from all over Israel to meet me on Mount Carmel. And bring the four hundred and fifty prophets of Baal and the four hundred prophets of Asherah, who eat at Jezebel's table." (1 Kings 18:18-19)

Ahab gathered the people and Baal's prophets as Elijah had directed, except the four hundred prophets of Asherah, Baal's female consort. [They were not allowed to go. This was probably because Jezebel would not let them go.] "Then in the presence of people and prophets, Elijah said to them, 'I am the only one of the Lord's prophets left, but Baal has four hundred and fifty. Get two bulls for us. Let them choose one for themselves, and let them cut it into pieces and put it on the wood but not set fire to it. I will prepare the other bull and put it on the wood but not set fire to it. Then you call on the name of your god, and I will call on the name of the Lord. The god who answers by fire – he is God.'" (1 Kings 18:22-24) This was agreeable to all, both the people and the Baal prophets. These prophets could hardly disagree to this testing by fire since they taught that the God of Israel was less powerful than the Baals.

These prophets agreed to go first. It was too late for them to back out. They could not afford to have the people see one lone prophet of the God of Israel win out over 450 prophets of the Baal's hands down. Also notice that there was already an altar for Baal worship in place on Mount Carmel. At any rate, 450 men could get a bull ready to be sacrificed much faster than one man. So it made sense for them to make their sacrifice first, which they proceeded to do.

The prophets of the Baal's danced around the altar from morning to noon pleading for Baal to send fire to burn up the sacrifice. At noon Elijah began to mock them suggesting their god might be asleep or be busy about other things. When the normal time for the evening sacrifice arrived, there was still no response from Baal. Throughout the day the prophets of Baal had been cutting and slashing themselves until their blood ran freely from their bodies and the place around their altar was a bloody mess. "Midday passed, and they continued their frantic prophesying until the time for the evening sacrifice. But there was no response, no one answered, no one paid attention." (1 Kings 18:29) Notice the scripture emphasizes their *prophesying*. This had been going on for hours. During all this time, not only was Ahab there but also all the people who had gathered from all over the northern kingdom, yet the scripture also points out that *no one paid attention*. At least six hours had passed, but Baal was not responding. The people who had gathered had other matters on their minds. The prophet's extreme measures and the spectacle presented by 450 men attempting for hours to get their god's attention did not even hold the people's attention after a while.

To get to the short of it, Elijah, after the people's patience had run out, in the name of the Lord reconstructed God's ruined altar using twelve stones. He placed wood on it, on which he laid his bull, cut in pieces. Then he had gallons and gallons of water repeatedly poured on the altar. The altar and the trench and ground around the altar were thoroughly drenched. Then in one brief prayer, offered only once, he asked God to respond, not even requesting that it be by fire. "Then the fire of the Lord fell and burned up the sacrifice, the wood, the stones and the soil, and also licked up the water in the trench. When all the people saw this, they fell prostrate and cried, "The Lord – He is God! The Lord – He is God!" (1 Kings 18:38-39)

But what about those 450 prophets of Baal? What did Elijah direct the people to do with them? Recall that in our review above of the fate of false prophets and prophets of other gods: they were all to be put to death. Some who read about Elijah's command that all these prophets be killed may think he was cruel and insensitive to human suffering. "Then Elijah commanded them, 'Seize the prophets of Baal. Don't let anyone get away!' They seized them, and Elijah had them brought down to the Kishon Valley and slaughtered there." (1 Kings 18:40) Their fate was exactly as God directed.

Now do you remember what God had told Elijah would happen when he met Ahab that second time? "Go and present yourself to Ahab, and I will send rain on the land." (1 Kings 18:1) At this point someone might be wondering why Ahab would be willing to do as Elijah had directed him. Ahab considered him to be his enemy and the one who was causing all the problems associated with a long famine, and in addition, had his troops out scouring the northern kingdom and all the adjacent kingdoms to find him. It should be evident that Elijah told Ahab at this second meeting that he would send rain and the famine on the land would be ended, but that it would hinge on gathering the people to Mount Carmel along with Baal's prophets. What I have just proposed as the reason Ahab did what Elijah asked is not recorded anywhere in this account of Elijah's relationship with the king, so I have no way to verify what I have just surmised.

Then Elijah himself, having assured Ahab that a heavy rain was indeed on the way and it was time for the king to have a meal, climbed to the very peak of Carmel and sent his servant to look out to sea. At this time of the year storms probably swept over the land from off the Mediterranean Sea bringing an abundance of rain, but Elijah bent down putting his face between his knees. When the servant returned he reported he had seen nothing. First Kings 18:43-46: "'Go look toward the sea,' he told his servant. And he went up and looked. 'There is nothing there,' he said. Seven times Elijah said, 'Go back.' The seventh time the servant reported, 'A cloud as small as a man's hand is rising from the sea.' So Elijah said, 'Go and tell Ahab, hitch up your chariot and go down before the rain stops you.' Meanwhile, the sky grew black with clouds, the wind rose, a heavy rain began and Ahab rode off to Jezreel. The power of the Lord came upon Elijah and, tucking his cloak into his belt, he ran ahead of Ahab all the way to Jezreel."

The question arises, why didn't Elijah go look for the cloud himself? Instead, as noted, he deliberately hid his eyes so he would not see what was happening at sea. It seems to me that God was telling Elijah he had done the job God gave him to do and now could expect God to carry out His part of the deal. It had required faith on the part of Elijah to face 450 prophets of the Baals and show their gods to be worthless. It would also take faith in the God of Israel to expect Him to bring an end to the famine with a heavy rain. By hiding his eyes Elijah took himself out of the picture making sure God would receive full credit for the rain. By sending his servant seven times to look for the rising cloud Elijah exhibited an unfaltering faith. Is not this the kind of faith all of God's people should have as we go about God's work?

Then God did something else that is surprising, at least to me. He empowered Elijah with the strength to run, on foot, ahead of Ahab who was riding in his chariot. Elijah stayed ahead of Ahab who no doubt had ordered his charioteer to go as fast as possible to reach Jezreel before the mud from the rain could clog up the chariot wheels This was a distance of close to twenty miles! But there is probably another reason.

As a result of the events on Carmel, the return of rain to the land and Elijah's run, it should have been very apparent to Ahab that Elijah was indeed God's true prophet. Ahab should have returned to his palace a changed man, having observed that what Elijah prophesied came to pass as predicted. He then should have set his wife straight; had all her prophets who worshipped Asheroth put to death, and destroyed Baal's temple, the altar he had built for Baal, the Baal stone and the Asherah pole. Instead, Ahab gave his wife a detailed account of everything he had witnessed, who then sent a message to Elijah that she would have his life by the very next day. Certainly Ahab knew about her threat to kill Elijah but did nothing to stop her. So how would Elijah avoid being killed by Jezebel's soldiers (who had already been killing some of God's other prophets at her command)?

"Elijah was afraid and ran for his life. When he came to Beersheba in Judah, he left his servant there, while he himself went a day's journey into the desert. He came to a broom tree, sat down under it and prayed that he might die. 'I have had enough, Lord,' he said. 'Take my life, I am no better than my ancestors.' Then he laid down under the tree and fell asleep." (1 Kings 19:3-5)

This formerly intrepid prophet, willing to take on 450 prophets of Baal, is now running again, not in front of a fast moving chariot, but this time for his life, afraid of a vengeful woman, Jezebel. Where did he go? He left the northern kingdom, going south to the southernmost location of the southern kingdom; to Beersheba, which the scripture reminds us is in Judah. However, he stops at Beersheba only long enough to drop off his servant before proceeding another day's journey south of the city, into the desert.

This flight away from Jezebel is the first recorded instance of Elijah going anywhere not directed by God. It is understandable that Elijah would want to get out of the northern kingdom where Jezebel, who sought his life, was in control. It also makes sense that he would not want to go into one of the Canaanite cities clustered around the Promised Land. Jezebel herself was a Canaanite. All these towns worshipped the Baal of that particular city. It would be easy for her and Ahab to have Elijah picked up and brought back to the northern kingdom. It is less apparent why Elijah would not feel safe staying in the southern kingdom.

During this period of Elijah's ministry, Asa was king of the southern kingdom. He was not on good terms with Ahab at this time and it seems unlikely, if requested, he would catch Elijah and send him back to

Jezreel and certain death. Elijah must have known no love was lost between the two kings, but the nation had not been divided that long and there were still some ties between the two houses. To add to Elijah's uncertainty, Asa's grandmother, Maacah, was the queen mother in Jerusalem about that time, and she had seen to it that an image of Asherah was made and installed in the temple in Jerusalem, even though Asa had instituted some reforms in the land favoring God. This devotion to Baal's consort by both Jezebel and Maacah gave the two women, though in different kingdoms, common ground. Who knows whether the two queen mothers might decide to persuade the two kings to turn Elijah over to Jezebel. It was a risk Elijah was evidently not willing to take. So he continued going south out of the southern kingdom. And he went in his own strength, not by the power of God as was the case when he ran in front of Ahab's chariot from Carmel to Jezreel (based on that run Elijah could probably be put in The Guinness Book of Records as having run the fastest mile of any man ever).

As noted above, Elijah told the Lord in essence that all he had done had not changed Baal worship one iota in the northern kingdom, and he had been kidding himself thinking it had. The statements he made indicates just how despondent he had become. He wants to give up but God still has a ministry for him. Look again at Elijah's remarks.

1 Kings 19:3-5: "Elijah was afraid and ran for his life. When he came to Beersheba in Judah, he left his servant there, while he himself went a day's journey into the desert. He came to a broom tree, sat down under it and prayed that he might die. 'I have had enough, Lord,' he said. 'Take my life; I am no better than my ancestors.' Then he laid down under the tree and fell asleep."

Instead of granting Elijah's wish, the Lord dealt with him patiently and gracefully. I think what we are seeing in his very unusual behavior is that Elijah had come to believe he had been calling the shots. Had he not faced 450 fervid prophets of Baal and gotten the best of them? Not only was Elijah exhausted physically at this point, he was being very self-centered, as though the outcome of his ministry for God depended solely on him. The only other prophet recorded as asking God to take his life was Jonah.

Jonah 4:3: "Now, O Lord, take away my life, for it is better for me to die than to live!" This occurred when Jonah realized God had spared Nineveh from destruction. Notice that both prophets thought they knew better than God. Jonah had said, "It is better for me to die." Elijah said, "I have had enough, Lord." It was not the right of either prophet to decide whether they needed to die or when. Only God decides that. Both prophets were out of order. Jonah, waiting to see what would happen to Nineveh, repeated his gaffe after God provided shade for him from the hot sun then sent a worm to eat the vine providing the shade, causing it to wither away, then sending a scorching east wind to discomfort Jonah.

God then patiently reminded His reluctant prophet that if he was so put out because of the action of a worm and a wind, should not God be concerned about the fate of 120,000 ignorant souls in Nineveh who repented, as well as their cattle? (Recall that the cattle were made to fast. They were not fed nor watered.) Jonah 3:6-9: "When the news reached the king of Nineveh, he rose from his throne, took off his royal robes, covered himself with sackcloth and sat down in the dust. Then he issued a proclamation in Nineveh: By the decree of the king and his nobles: 'Do not let any man or beast, herd or flock, taste anything; do not let them eat or drink. But let man and beast be covered with sackcloth. Let everyone call urgently on God. Let them give up their evil ways and their violence. Who knows? God may yet relent and with compassion turn from His fierce anger so that we will not perish.'"

The king said, "Who knows?" What a contrast with the two prophets of God who had thoughtlessly decided they knew what God should do and when he should do it. The king of Nineveh, not exactly what we would call a theologian, avoided playing God or telling Him how to conduct His business. Because the king and his subjects threw themselves on the mercy of God, this major Assyrian city was given another 150 years before its destruction. The city was destroyed in 712 BC. Jonah proclaimed his warning to them around 850 BC. Notice that God did not eliminate the coming destruction. He delayed it until all those in the city who had repented had died.

There are at least two other occasions when God pronounced disaster on each of the two kingdoms but when king and people humbled themselves before Him, He delayed the disaster. When Ahab repented (see 1 Kings 21:27-29), God told Elijah that because Ahab had humbled himself before Him, He would not bring disaster in his days but in the days of his son. In 2 Kings 22:11-20 when the book of the law was discovered in the temple and read to the king, Josiah realized that, since the days of their fathers, the nation had disobeyed God, breaking the covenant given to Moses at Horeb. Look at verses 19-20 as God speaks to Josiah, king of Judah, "Because your heart was responsive and you humbled yourself before the Lord when you heard what I have spoken against this place and its people, that they would become accursed and laid waste, and because you tore your robes and wept in my presence, I have heard you, declares the Lord. Therefore I will gather you to your fathers, and you will be buried in peace. Your eyes will not see all the disaster I am going to bring on this place." In all three cases, devastation was delayed until all those who humbled themselves had died. It doesn't take a rocket scientist to realize the value of a repentant heart in God's sight.

Elijah and Jonah were like a lot of us today to whom God has given a ministry. Too often we want to give up when we don't see the results we seek or expect, or when our timeframe for achieving *our* objectives is not met. Often when we think we see clearly what needs to be done, it isn't clear to others, and it is not unusual to encounter resistance, however well meaning, from others. As a result of all this, it is no wonder our faith often goes begging. Or we turn in on ourselves and cry in our beer because "I am the only one left and they are trying to get rid of me." The conclusions of both Elijah and Jonah were irrelevant and indicate their failure to understand that God's ways will always override man's ways.

Now our despondent prophet is about to be dealt with by the God who loves him and will help him to get back on track. From this time on until his miraculous departure from earth, Elijah's ministry reflects the service of a more mature prophet.

First Kings 19:5-9: "Then he lay down under the tree and fell asleep. All at once an angel touched him and said, 'Get up and eat.' He looked around, and there by his head was a cake of bread baked over hot coals, and a jar of water. He ate and drank and then lay down again. The angel of the Lord came back a second time and touched him and said, 'Get up and eat, for the journey is too much for you.' So he got up and ate and drank. Strengthened by that food, he traveled forty days and forty nights until he reached Horeb, the mountain of God. There he went into a cave and spent the night."

So the prophet whom God fed first by ravens at the Kerith Ravine, then by a poor widow at Zarephath, is now being fed by the angel of God under a broom tree in the desert! In fact, the angel provides Elijah with two meals so he will have the physical strength for his journey. Note that God does not chide or discourage Elijah for running from Jezebel. Nor are we told why the journey to Horeb (Mt. Sinai) took forty days, nor why there is no further reference to food during that time. There must have been, in the desert, some type of physical nourishment available but there was no manna. It is unlikely this trip was supposed to be a time of fasting for Elijah. God sent His angel to him for the express purpose of feeding him, telling him the journey was too much for him with no food. It is also unlikely Elijah moved from one place to another for the better part of forty days, not necessarily closer to Horeb, to evade any of Jezebel's soldiers who might still be looking for him even in the desert.

Whatever the reason, when he reached Horeb the word of God came to Elijah asking what he was doing there. First Kings 19:10-13: "He replied, 'I have been very zealous for the Lord God Almighty. The Israelites have rejected your covenant, broken down your altars, and put your prophets to death with the sword. I am the only one left, and now they are trying to kill me too.' The Lord said, 'Go out and stand on the mountain in the presence of the Lord, for the Lord is about to pass by.' Then a great and powerful wind tore the mountains apart and shattered the rocks before the Lord, but the Lord was not in the wind. After the wind there was an earthquake, but the Lord was not in the earthquake. After the earthquake came a fire, but the Lord was not in the fire. And after the fire came a gentle whisper. When Elijah heard it, he pulled his cloak over his face and went out and stood at the mouth of the cave. Then a voice said to him, "What are you doing here, Elijah?"

Then Elijah repeated exactly what he had told the Lord in response to His question. Essentially, that they have rejected *your* covenant, broken down *your* altars, put *your* prophets to death and I am the only one left and they are out to kill me. (And don't forget I'm *your* prophet also.) It seems that Elijah expected God to do something dramatic, given his emphasis on 'your.' How could God overlook all this blatant disobedience by Israel? Especially since they are trying to kill him.

God's delayed response to Israel's open disobedience to His covenant led many of His prophets, not just in the days of Elijah and Elisha but throughout the prophetic years from Samuel to Malachi, to prophesy severe judgment on both the northern and southern kingdoms if they continued to disobey their God.

After God had reminded Elijah that, in fact, he was not alone because there were seven thousand left in Israel who did not worship Baal, He told Elijah to get back in the saddle: 1) go to Damascus and anoint Hazael king over Aram, 2) anoint Jehu son of Nimshi king over Israel, and 3) anoint Elisha son of Shaphat from Abel Meholah to succeed him as prophet (see 1 Kings 19:15-18). It's interesting that Abel Meholah, Elisha's home town, was only about two miles directly across the Jordan River from the Kerith Ravine where Elijah had first hidden from Ahab after telling the king it was not going to rain until he said so. (Look at a map of that area for these places.)

Elijah found Elisha and threw his cloak around him. The significance of this action was unmistakable. Elisha, who was himself plowing in a field at the time along with eleven other teams of oxen and apparently from a well-to-do family, promptly killed his team of oxen, cooked them to provide a meal for the locals, bid his father and mother goodbye and then followed Elijah as his attendant (see 1 Kings 19:19-21). By emphasizing Elisha becoming Elijah's *attendant*, just after casting him as a prominent family member (overseeing the plowing of a large field – you don't use twelve plowing teams to do the backyard) preparing the fields for planting, it's plain Elisha was more accustomed to giving orders than being someone's *attendant*. Later on we shall see Elisha using both hats to his advantage as circumstances require. He served Elijah well, himself telling Hazael he would be the king of Aram and arranging to have Jehu anointed king over Israel. He was known as the one who poured water on Elijah's hands.

Elisha was well known in the southern as well as in the northern kingdom as suggested by an incident noted in 2 Kings 3:11-12. "But Jehoshaphat asked, 'Is there no prophet of the Lord here, that we may inquire of the Lord through him?' An officer of the king of Israel answered, 'Elisha, son of Shaphat is here. He used to pour water on the hands of Elijah.' Jehoshaphat said, 'The word of the Lord is with him.' So the king of Israel and Jehoshaphat and the king of Edom went down to him." As it turned out, it was Elisha who told Hazael he would be king of Aram. And it was a young prophet, his name not provided in the account, sent by Elisha with oil to anoint Jehu, son of Nimshi, an officer in Joram's army, to be the next king over Israel. Second Kings 9:6-10: "Jehu got up and went into the house. Then the prophet poured the oil on Jehu's head and declared, 'This is what the Lord, the God of Israel, says: I anoint you king over the Lord's people Israel. You are to destroy the house of Ahab your master, and I will avenge the blood of my servants the prophets and the blood of all the Lord's servants shed by Jezebel. I will cut off from Ahab every last male in Israel – slave or free. I will make the house of Ahab like the house of Jeroboam son of Nebat and like the house of Baasha son of Ahijah. As for Jezebel, dogs will devour her on the plot of ground at Jezreel, and no one will bury her.' Then he opened the door and ran." Jezebel was not the only wife of Ahab. He had seventy sons. Jehu was directed to kill all of Ahab's sons and his chief men, close friends, and his priests. (see 2 Kings 10:10-11)

We might be tempted to think at this point that Elijah's ministry is now finished, but not so. Elijah will no longer fear Jezebel who appears once more not to hunt for Elijah, but to help her husband rob Naboth of his vineyard next door to the palace. Once more the Lord directs Elijah to meet Ahab and deliver a message: "This is what the Lord says: Have you not murdered a man and seized his property? ...in the place where dogs licked up Naboth's blood, dogs will lick up your blood – yes yours!" (1 Kings 21:17-19) Then Ahab's fate is revealed to him. "'I am going to bring disaster on you. I will consume your descendants and cut off from Ahab every last male in Israel – slave or free. I will make your house like that of Jeroboam son of Nebat and that of Baasha son of Abijah, because you have provoked me to anger and have caused Israel to sin.' And also concerning Jezebel the Lord says: 'Dogs will devour Jezebel by the wall of Jezreel. Dogs will eat those belonging to Ahab who die in the city, and the birds of the air will feed on those who die in the country.'" (1 Kings 21:21-24)

Now comes a major surprise. We see a repentant Ahab! "When Ahab heard these words, he tore his clothes, put on sackcloth and fasted. He lay in sackcloth and went around meekly." And now another surprise! God tells Elijah that because Ahab humbled himself before Him, He will not bring this disaster in his day but will bring it on his house in the days of his son. (1 Kings 21:28) As noted above, repentance has great value in the sight of God and is always timely for the wicked.

Let us look now at the last major confrontation between Elijah and a king of Israel before Elijah is taken up to heaven in a whirlwind. Ahaziah son of Ahab had fallen in his house, severely injuring himself. Instead of inquiring from the God of Israel if he would live, he sent messengers to the Phoenician town of Ekron whose god was Baal-Zebub. This particular Baal was thought to be able to tell the future. An angel directed Elijah to meet the messengers and declare the king would die and had no business seeking an answer from a Baal as though there were no God in Israel. The messengers then went back and told the king Elijah said he would die from his injury.

Apparently where Elijah was staying was no secret to the king, who proceeded to send soldiers to get him. He is pictured as sitting on a hill, perhaps in the Carmel Range. "Then he sent to Elijah a captain with his company of fifty men. The captain went up to Elijah, sitting on the top of a hill, and said to him, 'Man of God, the king says, Come down!' Elijah answered the captain, 'If I am a man of God, may fire come down from heaven and consume you and your fifty men!' Then fire fell from heaven and consumed the captain and his men." (2 Kings 1:9-10) The king sent another captain and fifty men with the same result. This captain doubled down on the king's directive, telling Elijah 'This is what the king says.' The king himself intensified his order by adding 'at once.' However, it is not written that this captain went up to Elijah, just that he directed him to come down at once. Finally, a third captain with fifty men was

76

dispatched. This time the third captain, a bit apprehensive to say the least, went up and fell on his knees before Elijah, "'Man of God.' he begged, 'please have respect for my life and the lives of these fifty men, your servants! See, fire has fallen from heaven and consumed the first two captains and all their men. But now have respect for my life and the lives of these fifty men, your servants.'" (2 Kings 1:13-14) Directed by the angel of the Lord, Elijah went with this captain to the king and told him he would never leave his bed but would die because he had sent messengers to consult Baal Zebub instead of the God of Israel.

Initially it may seem a bit repulsive that one hundred and two men die by fire from heaven simply because they order Elijah to go with them to see the king. However, we should realize what little regard, if any, the king, and the northern kingdom, had for the God of heaven and earth at this time. When Elijah met the king this was his question to him. "This is what the Lord says, 'Is it because there is no God in Israel for you to consult that you have sent messengers to consult Baal-Zebub, the god of Ekron?'" The king had such contempt for the Lord that he ranked Him below the Baals, especially the god of Ekron. I'm sure the king believed that Israel had its own god. That made his snub even worse. He treated God as just another god, like the Baals, but inferior. Consider what an affront to God this was. Don't forget that God chose Israel to be the showcase of His glory and majesty so all the other nations would realize there was no god but one, that of Israel, His chosen possession. Had Israel obeyed God He would have blessed the nation to such an extent that all the other nations would have realized there was no god except the God of Israel.

"If you pay attention to these laws and are careful to follow them, then the Lord your God will keep His covenant of love with you, as He swore to your forefathers. He will love you and bless you and increase your numbers. He will increase the fruit of your womb, the crops of your land – your grain, new wine and oil – the calves of your herds and the lambs of your flocks in the land that He swore to your forefathers to give you. You will be blessed more than any other people; none of your men or women will be childless, nor any of your livestock without young. The Lord will keep you free from every disease. He will not inflict on you the horrible diseases you knew in Egypt, but He will inflict them on all who hate you. You must destroy all the peoples the Lord your God gives over to you. Do not look on them with pity and do not serve their gods, for that will be a snare to you." (Deuteronomy 7:12-16)

With this in mind, consider what a despicable insult to God this king committed when he sent messengers to consult the god of Ekron about his illness. Nothing is ever said about any Baal god loving his worshippers, nor is there any exhortation to be holy attributed to any lifeless idol. Nowhere in scripture is Baal credited by his prophets with bringing a dead person back to life and under no conditions had any Baal ever been able to call down fire from the sky for any purpose.

Baal's prophets, on the only occasion recorded, could not get their worthless gods to send fire from heaven to consume a sacrifice to him even after six hours of yelling, cavorting around their altar and cutting themselves. Witness the episode at Mt. Carmel where Baal's prophets couldn't even get him to light a fire on their sacrificial altar. The fire from heaven called down by Elijah on the captains and their soldiers punctuated the worthlessness of the Baals and emphasized God's declaration that He would destroy His chosen nation if they made any kind of idol to worship like all the other nations. "After you have had children and grandchildren and have lived in the land a long time – if you then become corrupt and make any kind of idol, doing evil in the eyes of the Lord your God and provoking Him to anger, I call heaven and earth as witnesses against you this day that you will quickly perish from the land that you are crossing the Jordan to possess. You will not live there long but will certainly be destroyed. The Lord will scatter you among the peoples, and only a few of you will survive among the nations to which the Lord will drive you." (Deuteronomy 4:25-27)

But there may still be a question about why the soldiers were consumed in the fire. Weren't the soldiers simply obeying orders? What evil had they done? Their captains had been charged to bring this prophet of God to the king, period. Any answer we might give will probably not be completely satisfactory. Look at the situation this way. Was it only the kings and officials who were forbidden to worship idols? Thankfully the scripture is very clear in this respect. "Carefully follow the terms of this covenant, so that you may prosper in everything you do. All of you are standing today in the presence of the Lord your God – your leaders and chief men, your elders and officials, and *all the other men of Israel*, together with your children and your wives, and the aliens living in your camps who chop your wood and carry your water. You are standing here in order to enter into a covenant with the Lord your God, a covenant the Lord is making with you this day and sealing with an oath, to confirm you this day as His people, that He may be your God as He promised you and as He swore to your fathers, Abraham, Isaac and Jacob. I am making this covenant, with its oath, not only with you who are standing here with us today in the presence of the Lord our God but also *with those who are not here today*." (Deuteronomy 29:9-15, *emphasis mine*)

"Make sure there is no man or woman, clan or tribe among you today whose heart turns away from the Lord your God to go and worship the gods of those nations; make sure there is no root among you that produces such bitter poison." (Deuteronomy 29:18)

Based on the scriptures just cited we understand that everyone in the nation was responsible for obeying God's covenant, including the soldiers. They were also under God's orders to worship Him and no other. Because the fire consumed the soldiers they must be considered guilty of not obeying the covenant and saw no problem with ordering a man of God to jump when they said, "Frog." Only the third captain humbled himself before God, kneeling and appealing for mercy to Elijah for himself and his fifty men. Neither of the first two captains expressed any concern for the welfare of their men. The third captain's humility also saved the lives of his fifty men, even though they probably believed no differently than the first hundred soldiers.

After talking about Elijah calling down fire from heaven, the scripture switches immediately to Elijah himself being called up to heaven in a whirlwind. Prior to crossing the Jordan River, Elijah and Elisha visited groups of God's prophets at Bethel and Jericho. At each location Elijah admonished Elisha to stay there while he went on. Elisha would not agree to let Elijah proceed alone. When they finally reached the river, Elijah rolled up his robe and struck the water, which divided, allowing them to cross the Jordan on dry ground. After crossing, they walked on together.

All the prophets they had visited and Elisha knew that Elijah would be leaving the earth that day. One of the heartwarming things about this incident was the respect, love and commitment each man had for the other. Staying with Elijah on his journey from Gilgal to the Jordan meant Elisha must walk about fifteen miles further than if he had stayed at Gilgal as instructed. Elijah must have been grateful and very pleased to see his servant fully devoted to him to the very last day. In fact, once over the Jordan River, he asked Elisha what he could do for him before he was taken from him. The offer itself was unusual to say the least. The response was even more remarkable and illustrated what a close bond they had formed; the one the master, the other the servant.

A close review of these last moments before Elijah departed are in order. "When they had crossed, Elijah said to Elisha, 'Tell me, what can I do for you before I am taken from you?' 'Let me inherit a double portion of your spirit.' Elisha replied [γενηθήτω δὴ διπλᾶ ἐν πνεύματί σου ἐπ᾽ ἐμέ]." (2 Kings 2:9 Lxx). The Greek translation of the Hebrew text is given here for those who may be interested in comparing its basic meaning to the various English translations.

"'You have asked a difficult thing' Elijah said, 'yet if you see me when I am taken from you, it will be yours–otherwise not.' As they were walking along and talking together, suddenly a chariot of fire and horses of fire appeared and separated the two of them, and Elijah went up to heaven in a whirlwind. Elisha saw this and cried out, 'My father! My father! The chariots and horsemen of Israel!' And Elisha saw him no more. Then he took hold of his own clothes and tore them apart. He picked up the cloak that had fallen from Elijah and went back and stood on the bank of the Jordan. Then he took the cloak that had fallen from him and struck the water with it. 'Where now is the Lord, the God of Elijah?' he asked. When he struck the water, it divided to the right and to the left, and he crossed over." (2 Kings 2:9-14)

A natural question arises at this point. Why would Elisha's request be granted only if Elisha saw Elijah when he was taken? What will there be about Elijah's leaving that will ensure Elisha getting a double share– or portion–of Elijah's spirit? Many commentators have said or implied this refers to a first born son receiving a double inheritance of his father's estate at his death. Considering that Elisha called out "My father! My father! The chariots and horsemen of

Israel!" (1 Kings 2:12), it might seem to confirm the idea of father–elder son succession (see Deuteronomy 21:17). But Elisha is not Elijah's son. Crying out "My father!" most likely refers to the great respect Elisha had for Elijah.

This phrase is used two more times in 2 Kings where Deuteronomy 21:17 clearly does not apply. Second Kings 6:20-21: "After they entered the city, Elisha said, 'Lord, open the eyes of these men so they can see.' Then the Lord opened their eyes and they looked, and there they were, inside Samaria. When the king of Israel saw them, he asked Elisha, 'Shall I kill them, *my father*? Shall I kill them?'" (*emphasis mine*) 2 Kings 13:10; 14: "In the thirty-seventh year of Joash king of Judah, Jehoash son of Jehoahaz became king of Israel in Samaria, and he reigned sixteen years... Now Elisha was suffering from the illness from which he died. Jehoash king of Israel went down to see him and wept over him. '*My father! My father!*' he cried. 'The chariots and horsemen of Israel!'" (*emphasis mine*) To my knowledge this phrase appears nowhere else in the scriptures.

Ruling out the firstborn son's double inheritance theory to explain this situation brings us back to Elijah's warning, "If you see me when I am taken from you, it will be yours–otherwise not."

So put yourself in Elisha's place. No human had ever seen anyone taken up bodily into heaven, in a whirlwind, and accompanied by a chariot of fire and horses of fire. What effect would seeing this have had on you? Think you would have gone back across the Jordan River dispirited and sorrowful? Elisha had just been treated to a display of God's mighty power. Chariots and horses spoke of an army. The Lord Almighty was the God of the heavenly hosts. Who or what could withstand chariots and horses of fire? Elisha did not see any *horsemen* of fire but he cried out "the chariots and *horsemen* of Israel." So *God opened the eyes of Elisha so he would see the chariot and horses of fire* accompany Elijah to heaven. This was an honor guard for this great prophet assuring him he would arrive safely in spite of hostile heavenly forces. Ephesians 6:12: "For your struggle is not against flesh and blood, but against the rulers, against the authorities, against the powers of this dark world and against the spiritual forces of evil in the heavenly realms." This was an overwhelming revelation of the almighty power of the God of Israel, Ruler of the hosts of heaven. With a God like this, what did Elisha have to fear as he took up where Elijah left off? Later, when the Aramean king sent special forces with chariots and horses (not of fire, of course) to surround Dothan and capture Elisha, he asked God to open the eyes of his terrified servant so he could also see *God's chariots and horses of fire.* At that point the servant's spiritual eyes were opened and he saw the hills full of chariots and horses of fire gathered around Elisha.

From this point on Elisha walked without fear of kings or queens or their kingdoms. The miracles he performed were also known by all the sons of God's prophets as well as kings and palace officials, and respect for him permeated not only the northern kingdom but Aram as well.

And if we are satisfied that we have now circumscribed everything that was to flow from this double portion anointing of Elijah's spirit, we should recall the words of Paul, "Now to Him who is able to do immeasurably more than all we ask or imagine, according to His power that is at work within us, to Him be glory in the church and in Christ Jesus throughout all generations, forever and ever! (Ephesians 3:20-21) So with the expectation that God will do more than double up his spirit, we should expand our view to include everything that happened during Elisha's ministry. Yep, sure enough, Elisha's 54 years of ministry were twice as long as Elijah's 27 years of ministry. If you doubt this, check the timelines of these two prophets in a study bible timeline. How long did the famine in Elijah's ministry last? Three and a half years. James 5:17: "Elijah was a man just like us. He prayed earnestly that it would not rain, and it did not rain on the land for three and a half years." Second Kings 8:1: "Now Elisha had said to the woman whose son he had restored to life, 'Go away with your family and stay for a while wherever you can because the Lord has decreed a famine in the land that will last seven years.'"

Counting all the miraculous acts or events in both ministries, we find Elisha's are twice those of Elijah. Last but certainly not least was the raising from the dead ministry of these two prophets. When the widow's son died, God raised him back to life through the intervention of Elijah. 1 Kings 17:22-23: "The Lord heard Elijah's cry, and the boy's life returned to him, and he lived. Elijah picked up the child and carried him down from the room into the house. He gave him to his mother and said, 'Look, your son is alive!'"

God also used Elisha to restore life to the Shunammite woman's son. Second Kings 4:20-21; 32-36: "After the servant had lifted him up and carried him to his mother, the boy sat on her lap until noon, and then he died. She went up and laid him on the bed of the man of God, then shut the door and went out. When Elisha reached the house, there was the boy lying dead on his couch. He went in, shut the door on the two of them and prayed to the Lord. Then he got on the bed and lay upon the boy, mouth to mouth, eyes to eyes, hand to hands. [*This must be the first known case of CPR*] He stretched himself out upon him; the boy's body grew warm. Elisha turned away and walked back and forth in the room and then got on the bed and stretched out upon him once more. The boy sneezed seven times and opened his eyes. Elisha summoned Gehazi and said, 'Call the Shunammite.' And he did. When she came, he said, 'Take your son.'"

So now we have Elijah giving life once and Elisha giving life once, not twice, as we may have thought would happen, in keeping with the double portion theme bestowed on Elisha when he began his ministry. There also seems to be a disconnect regarding the total number of years each prophet served. In reference to the timeline of the two prophets, Elijah served from 879 BC to 852 BC, or 27 years. Elisha is recorded as serving from 852 BC to 796 BC, or 52 years, before he died of an illness (if my math is working right). This is short by two years of a double portion of Elijah's time in ministry. However, we find something extremely interesting when we consider the scripture relating to Elisha's death. Second Kings 13:20-21: "Elisha died and was buried." There are just five words in the first sentence of the English translation; only six words in the LXX. There are no details about where he was buried or in what kind of tomb or burial site, nor who buried him.

The Greek text says only 'they' buried him. The NIV and NKJV resort to the passive verb, 'was buried.'

Then, still in verse 20, the next sentence: "Now Moabite raiders used to enter the country every spring," seems to have nothing to do at all with Elisha's death and burial. However, notice what happened next, in verse 21: "Once while some Israelites were burying a man, suddenly they saw a band of raiders; so they threw the man's body into Elisha's tomb. When the body touched Elisha's bones, the man *came to life* and stood up on his feet. Bingo! Two raisings to life for Elisha to one for Elijah!

Well, someone might say, "Okay, you took care of that problem but what about Elisha's ministry falling short of doubling Elijah's by two years?" The scripture here makes it plain that those who threw the dead man's body into Elisha's tomb had no idea whose tomb or burial site it was. We are left to infer it was the closest one, allowing them to leave the area quickly before the Moabite raiders discovered them. The point is made that the dead man came back to life only after his body had touched Elisha's *bones*. Those who threw the dead man into Elisha's tomb had no concern whether the body touched anything. They were only interested in putting distance between themselves and the raiders, but by telling us about the body touching Elisha's bones we know for a fact he had been dead more than one year. The Israelites did not embalm or cremate their dead. After one year, allowing time for the flesh to decay and turn to dust, the bones were usually gathered and often placed together in separate locations. Since Elisha's bones had already been gathered, we will take it for granted he had been dead two years, increasing the length of his ministry to 54 years, making it twice that of Elijah and thus preserving the double portion theme. Only Almighty God, as usual doing more than we would even think to ask or imagine, could have brought about such an unlikely scenario to honor His Word. It is evident that we should all come into His presence daily with overflowing gratitude and thanksgiving for 1) His love and 2) respect for His ways. Nothing is too hard for God. He loves to bless His children.

The following account, during Elisha's ministry, relates the story of Naaman, an Aramean general. "Now Naaman was commander of the army of the King of Aram. He was a great man in the sight of his master and highly regarded, because through him the Lord had given victory to Aram. He was a valiant soldier, but he had leprosy." (2 Kings 5:1) He learned about Elisha through a young Israelite girl, taken captive earlier by Aram raiders and placed in Naaman's household to serve his wife. The girl had told his wife he should see the prophet in Samaria who would cure him of his skin disease (see 2 Kings

5:2-3). When Naaman related this to the king, he sent him to the King of Israel with a letter stating, in part, "With this letter I am sending my servant Naaman to you so that you may cure him of his leprosy." (2 Kings 5:6)

When Naaman left, he took with him ten talents of silver, (about 750 pounds) 6,000 shekels of gold, (about 150 pounds) and ten sets of clothing. This was a big deal involving a very important man who carried out his responsibilities at the highest levels of government. He was determined to pay his way. He had been given a referral by one king to another king. What he really needed was a referral to a specialist (Elisha), not a generalist! (pun intended) When the King of Israel read the letter Naaman presented to him, he thought the King of Aram was trying to pick a fight with him. "As soon as the King of Israel read the letter, he tore his robes and said, 'Am I God? Can I kill and bring back to life? Why does this fellow send someone to me to be cured of leprosy? See how he is trying to pick a quarrel with me!'" (2 Kings 5:7) Elisha, hearing the king had torn his robes, directed the king to send Naaman to him.

"So Naaman went with his horses and chariots and stopped at the door of Elisha's house. Elisha sent a messenger to say to him, 'Go, wash yourself seven times in the Jordan, and your flesh will be restored and you will be cleansed.' But Naaman went away angry and said, 'I thought that he would surely come out to me and stand and call on the name of the Lord, his God, wave his hand over the spot and cure me of my leprosy. Are not Abana and Pharpar, the rivers of Damascus, better than any of the waters of Israel? Couldn't I wash in them and be cleansed?' [*The prophet had not so much as come to the door to talk to the general*] So he turned and went off in a rage." (2 Kings 5:9-12) But as he was leaving, his servants convinced him to do as directed. "So he went down and dipped himself in the Jordan seven times, as the man of God had told him, and his flesh was restored and became clean like that of a young boy. Then Naaman and all his attendants went back to the man of God. He stood before him and said, 'Now I know that there is no God in all the world except in Israel. Please accept now a gift from your servant.'" (2 Kings 5:14-15) Elisha refused his gifts despite Naaman's urging, and on parting his last words to Elisha were "…your servant will never again make burnt offerings and sacrifices to any other god but the Lord." (2 Kings 5:17)

Beyond this encounter and subsequent healing of the imperial Aramean general, he is not mentioned again until Luke 4:27, "And there were many in Israel with leprosy in the time of Elisha the prophet, yet not one of them was cleansed–only Naaman the Syrian."

A comparison begs to be made between the poor widow of Zarephath and the commanding general of the Aramean army. 1) Elijah was ordered to go to the home of the widow of Zarephath who had no food or funds.   2) The proud general, with lavish gifts, was sent to Elisha instead of Elisha being sent to the general.   3) Elijah, in person at their first meeting, required the widow to prepare food first for himself then for her and her son. Elisha had his messenger direct the general to wash himself seven times in the Jordan.   4) Elisha would not speak to the general in person, an obvious snub to a man accustomed to giving orders to subordinates without even having to be present in person. Had the widow refused to cook for Elijah she would not have had food for the family and would have faced death by starvation. Had the general continued to refuse to do as he was told, he would not have been cured of leprosy. 5) The widow had nothing to offer Elijah except a sparse room in her house, not exactly like living at a Marriott. The general brought large sums of money and many changes of clothing, arriving at Elisha's house in an impressive manner with attendants, chariots, horses, an imperial attitude and the method (so he thought) all worked out in his mind by which he would be healed. "I thought he would wave his hands over my leprous flesh, calling on the name of his God, and I would be cleansed."

A premier prophet sent to an unnamed widow with no food or money; a proud general loaded down with millions in gifts sent to a prophet in Israel: astoundingly, with the same basic result for both: the widow: *"Now I know* the word of the Lord is the truth!"* The general: *"Now I know* the truth; there is no god in all the world except in Israel." The general realized what the truth portended in a flash. The lives of both were revolutionized. Israel was the only nation on earth which realized there was only one God and that He was not just one of the local gods but the Creator of the entire universe!

Later Israel would completely subvert the truth of one almighty God, as accused by Jeremiah 2:27-28, "They say to wood, you are my father, and to stone, you gave me birth. They have turned their backs to me and not their faces; yet when they are in trouble, they say, come and save us! Where then are the gods you made for yourselves? Let them come if they can save you when you are in trouble! For *you have as many gods as you have towns*, O Judah." Just like the other nations.

These two examples above point out that seeking and embracing the truth is an absolute requirement for Christians. God values those who seek the *truth about God to the point that He will either send someone who will verify the truth, or will send someone with the truth to the person seeking the truth.* Either way it is obvious God loves and works in the behalf of those who seek Him. The poor widow was willing to give Elijah, whom she had never seen before, the last of her food. The general repudiated his proud spirit and was willing to humble himself (1 Peter 5:5) and with contrition do exactly as Elisha directed. On that day a new word entered the general's vocabulary: *"Please."* Check out verses 15 and 17.

CHAPTER 7

Jesus and Judas

The treasurer of Jesus' group of twelve apostles, Judas Iscariot, was a thief! John 12:3-6: "Then Mary took about a pint of pure nard, an expensive perfume, and poured it on Jesus' feet and wiped His feet with her hair. And the house was filled with the fragrance of the perfume. But one of His disciples, Judas Iscariot, who was later to betray Him, objected, 'Why wasn't this perfume sold and the money given to the poor? It was worth a year's wages.' He did not say this because he cared about the poor but because he was a thief: as keeper of the money bag, he used to help himself to what was put into it."

Questions arise: why did the Lord permit Judas to be the treasurer? Did He not know Judas helped himself to the money in the bag? And why would Jesus choose Judas in the first place to be one of the twelve, if He was already aware that he would betray Him?

Listen to the scripture, John 6:64; 70-71: "'Yet there are some of you who do not believe.' For Jesus had known from the beginning which of them did not believe and who would betray him. Then Jesus replied, 'Have I not chosen you, the twelve? Yet one of you is a devil.'" In this context devil probably is best translated 'slanderer' or 'adversary.' Jesus does not mean to say Judas is himself Satan, prince of the demons, or that there are many Satans. John makes this clear in John 13:2; 21; and 27: "The evening meal was being served, and the devil had already prompted Judas Iscariot, son of Simon, to betray Jesus. After He had said this, Jesus was troubled in spirit and testified, 'I tell you the truth, one of you is going to betray me.' As soon as Judas took the bread, Satan entered into him. 'What you are about to do, do quickly,' Jesus told him, but no one at the meal understood why Jesus said this to him. Since Judas had charge of the money, some thought Jesus was telling him to buy what was needed for the feast, or to give something to the poor. As soon as Judas had taken the bread, he went out. And it was night."

Other scriptures give us a sense of Judas' compelling greed for money and emphasize the horrible consequences of a deliberate betrayal of the Son of Man into the hands of those who sought to kill Him. Matthew 26:14: "Then one of the twelve – the one called Judas Iscariot – went to the chief priests and asked, 'What are you willing to give me if I hand Him over to you?' So they counted out for him thirty silver coins. From then on Judas watched for an opportunity to hand Him over. Mark 14:20: "'It is one of the twelve,' He replied, 'one who dips bread into the bowl with me. The Son of Man will go just as it is written about Him. But woe to that man who betrays the Son of Man! It would be better for him if he had not been born.'"

This last statement about Judas is the only time Jesus ever said such a thing about anyone. Not even against the Pharisees or the Sadducees (most of them teachers of the law or scribes) did Jesus pronounce such an indictment. To those who cause one of the little ones who believe in Jesus to sin, He said, "It would be better for him to have a large millstone hung around his neck and to be drowned in the depths of the sea." (Matthew 18:6) But this is a far cry from declaring, "It would have been better had he not been born."

While an evening meal was being served, just before the Passover Feast, Jesus made this comment to the twelve: "I am not referring to all of you, I know those I have chosen. But this is to fulfill the scripture. 'He who shares my bread has lifted up his heel against me.'" (John 13:18) Also, see Matthew 26:23-24: "Jesus replied, 'The one who has dipped his hand into the bowl with me will betray me. The Son of Man will go just as it is written about Him. But woe to that man who betrays the Son of Man! It would be better for him if he had not been born." In both of these scriptures, Jesus refers to Psalm 41:9: "Even my close friend, whom I trusted, he who shared my bread, has lifted up his heel against me." Jesus makes it clear that He now tolerates Judas, once his best boyhood friend, in order that the Old Testament scripture about the two of them would be fulfilled. In Jesus' day there was no worse shame than for someone sharing the food of another to betray him or in some way to endanger him. Hence Jesus' remark about Judas dipping his hand in the bowl with Jesus identified him as such a man.

That Judas would be spoken of in the Psalms is a surprise to many Christians and, unfortunately, also to many pastors today. For this reason many have no idea how wicked this man was and why he would arrange for Jesus to be arrested by the temple police of the high priest. Matthew 26:45-49: "Then He returned to the disciples and said to them, 'Are you still sleeping and resting? Look, the hour is near, and the Son of Man is betrayed into the hands of sinners. Rise, let us go! Here comes my betrayer!' While He was still speaking, Judas, one of the twelve, arrived. With him was a large crowd armed with swords and clubs, sent from the chief priests and the elders of the people. Now the betrayer had arranged a signal with them. 'The one I kiss is the man; arrest him.' Going at once to Jesus, Judas said, 'Greetings Rabbi!' and kissed Him."

With that done, Judas fulfilled his agreement to betray Jesus for thirty silver coins. Is it any wonder that Jesus called Judas the one doomed to destruction: "None have been lost except the one doomed to destruction so that the scripture would be fulfilled." (John 17:12) The outcome of Judas' betrayal is summarized in Matthew 27:1-4: "Early in the morning, all the chief priests and the elders of the people came to the decision to put Jesus to death. They bound Him, led him away and handed Him over to Pilate, the governor. When Judas, who had betrayed Him, saw that Jesus was condemned, he was seized with remorse and returned the thirty silver coins to the chief priests and elders. 'I have sinned,' he said, 'for I have betrayed innocent blood.' 'What is that to us?' they replied. 'That's your responsibility.' So Judas threw the money into the temple and left. Then he went away and hanged himself."

Jesus' condemnation was completely contrary to what Judas' thought would happen. He had thought that Jesus, on being arrested, would stop dithering around, announce His kingship, set up rule in Jerusalem, throw out the Roman government, and install the twelve in official positions throughout the nation with great authority. Instead Jesus permitted Himself to be condemned to death. He made no defense at all. Then, as noted in the Old Testament, "They took the thirty silver coins, the price set on Him by the people of Israel, and they used them to buy the potter's field, as the Lord commanded me." (see Matthew 27:9-10)

So let us locate these scriptures in the Psalms that must be fulfilled. To do this, we now go to Acts 1:15-20: "In those days Peter stood up among the believers (a group numbering about a hundred and twenty) and said, 'Brothers, the scripture had to be fulfilled which the Holy Spirit spoke long ago through the mouth of David concerning Judas, who served as guide for those who arrested Jesus – he was one of our number and shared in this ministry.' (With the reward he got for his wickedness, Judas bought a field; there he fell headlong, his body burst open and all his intestines spilled out. Everyone in Jerusalem heard about this, so they called that field in their language Akeldama, that is, Field of Blood). 'For,' said Peter, 'it is written in the book of Psalms, May His place be deserted; let there be no one to dwell in it, and, May another take his place of leadership.'" These are quotes from Psalms 69 and 109. Three other Psalms (41, 42, 55) also refer to Judas. The first Psalm referenced by Peter is 69:25, but to understand the context and verify Peter's referral we must read Psalm

69:19-28: "You know how I am scorned, disgraced and shamed; all my enemies are before you. Scorn has broken my heart and has left me helpless; I looked for sympathy, but there was none, for comforters, but I found none. They put gall in my food and gave me vinegar for my thirst." This applies directly to Jesus and describes the wickedness of all who treated Jesus this way. Peter puts Judas in this group and changes the third person plural to the third person singular in the psalm so that 'they' becomes 'he' or 'him/his'. To continue, "May the table set before them become a snare; may their eyes be darkened so they cannot see, and their backs be bent forever. Pour out your wrath on them; let your fierce anger overtake them. May their *place* (greek *epaulis*) be deserted, let there be no one to dwell in their tents. For they persecute those you wound and talk about the pain of those you hurt. Charge them with crime after crime; do not let them share your salvation. May they be blotted out of the book of life and not be listed among the righteous." Remember the word *epaulis;* translated into English as 'place' in Acts 1:20, and used only once here in the New Testament.

Still looking at Peter's use of Psalms regarding Judas, he then cites Psalm 109:8: "May another take his place of leadership." To understand the context see Psalms 109:6-10: "Appoint an evil man to oppose him; let an accuser stand at his right hand. When he is tried, let him be found guilty, and may his prayers condemn him. May his days be few; may another take his place of leadership." The English translation of the NIV does not adequately deal with the Greek text in this verse. "Ein episkopein autou labeto heteros" may best be translated "May another take his leadership ministry." There is no word for 'place' in this verse and no sense that his position was an 'office.'

We will come back to the Psalms already cited, but in order to sharpen our focus on how the relationship of Jesus and Judas came about in the first place, let's try to find out when and where they first met. If we can do this, some of the mystery surrounding this most unusual pairing of men in the entire Bible should clear up.

Let's start with John 6:70-71: "Then Jesus replied, 'Have I not chosen you, the twelve? Yet one of you is a devil!' (He meant Judas, the son of Simon Iscariot, who, though one of the twelve, was later to betray Him.)" The reference to the son of Simon Iscariot most likely gives us the name of the town or village Judas' father came from. Iscariot means 'man of Kerioth.' Two towns by this name are located in the territory allotted to the tribe of Judah. (Carson, page 304) Matthew 10:4 refers to 'Judas Iscariot.' It seems obvious Judas is identified here as being from the Tribe of Judah, the same tribe as Jesus. Had 'Judas

Iscariot' meant that Judas was the son of Iscariot, then it probably would read 'Judas the son of Iscariot.' Being from the same tribe may also tell us how they first met.

When the Israelite men came to the three feasts they were required to attend in Jerusalem every year, they probably marched around the temple area by their tribes. Think about what church members do today when they go to a conference out of town. When seating themselves in the conference room, they tend to sit together. Let us refer back to Psalm 55:13-14. It is not too hard to think that two enthusiastic young men, both from the tribe of Judah, might lead the way in a throng of singing joyful men in procession around the temple area. See Psalm 42:4: "These things I remember as I pour out my soul [on the tree]; how I used to go with the multitude, leading the procession to the house of God, with shouts of joy and thanksgiving among the festive throng." Psalm 68:24-27 gives further credibility to what I have suggested: "Your procession has come into view, O God, the procession of my God and King into the sanctuary. In front are the singers, after them the musicians; with them are the maidens playing tambourines. Praise God in the great congregation; praise the Lord in the assembly of Israel. There is the little Tribe of Benjamin, leading them, there the great throng of Judah's princes [clan leaders], and there the princes of Zebulun and Naphtali." What a brief but revealing picture of the festive crowd we saw spoken of in Psalm 42:4. Then compare this with Psalm 55:13-14, along with Psalm 41:9, where Jesus speaks of Judas as his 'close friend,' whom He trusted, and with whom he *once* enjoyed sweet fellowship as they walked with the throng at the house of God. In saying *once* we are to be reminded that sweet fellowship did not continue after Judas had been chosen one of the twelve. In fact the only conversation on record between Jesus and Judas came at the evening meal before the Passover feast, when Jesus acknowledged Judas would betray Him and then told him, "What you are about to do, do quickly," and then again when Judas confronted Him on the mount of Olives to identify Him, with a kiss, to the temple police he had brought along to arrest Jesus.

Why did Judas arrange the Lord's arrest? Nothing in the Synoptics or John's gospel indicate Judas had a dislike for Jesus. In fact, Judas probably had great respect for Jesus. Was it just for the money? Does the betrayal indicate Judas had a fundamental difference of opinion about Jesus than the other eleven Apostles? Hardly. The scriptures indicate that all twelve of them completely misunderstood Jesus' mission as God's Messiah. Luke 18:31-34: "Jesus took the twelve aside and told them, 'We are going up to Jerusalem, and everything that is written by the prophets about the

105

Son of Man will be fulfilled. He will be handed over to the Gentiles. They will mock Him, insult Him, spit on Him, flog Him and kill Him. On the third day He will rise again.' The disciples did not understand any of this. [Rising on the third day did not seem to register at all.] Its meaning was hidden from them, and they did not know what He was talking about." Matthew 19:25-27: "When the disciples heard this, they were greatly astonished and asked, 'Who then can be saved?' Jesus looked at them and said, 'With man this is impossible, but with God all things are possible.' Peter answered him, 'We have left everything to follow you! What then will there be for us?' John 12:16: "At first his disciples did not understand all this. Only after Jesus was glorified did they realize that these things had been written about Him and that they had done these things to Him."

Judas had this misunderstanding of Jesus' Messiahship in common with the other eleven apostles. And he had something else in common with them. It is obvious that they all were expecting to get the VIP treatment when Jesus had kicked out the Roman government and began to rule the nation from Jerusalem. Peter's question, "What will there be for us?" expressed what they all were looking forward to. The kingdom they were all looking for was a return of the Davidic kingdom, but under Jesus' rule. Acts 1:6: "So when they met together, they asked Him, 'Lord are you at this time going to *restore* the kingdom to Israel?'"

Here is a very revealing incident in this regard: "Then the mother of Zebedee's sons (James and John, who wanted to call down fire from heaven on a Samaritan village) came to Jesus with her sons and, kneeling down, asked a favor of Him. 'What is it you want?' He asked. She said, 'Grant that one of these two sons of mine may sit at your right and the other at your left in your kingdom.'" (Matthew 20:20-21) Now notice the response from the ten (including Judas) when they hear about this. "When the ten heard about this, they were indignant with the two brothers." So once again Jesus tries to explain to all of them, Judas included, that the kingdom does not operate in accordance with worldly principles but through submissive and humble service to others. This principle of glad and humble service to others is beautifully brought out in the parable Jesus tells in Matthew 20:1-16, directly occasioned by the disciples' mistaken ideas of greatness in the kingdom.

Although Judas (time after time called 'one of the twelve') understood Jesus no better than any of the others, he differed from all the others in that he did not want to wait for the expected elevation to VIP status that the twelve would enjoy when Jesus made up His mind to start the ball rolling. To Judas' bewilderment, Jesus was evading His responsibilities as the Messiah.

Another reason for being so impatient with the Lord was the expense of the elaborate home he had or was building for his wife and children. Judas had a family? Where is that mentioned in the scriptures? Look in Psalms 109:8-15: "May his days be few; may another take his place of leadership [leadership ministry]. May his *children* be fatherless and his *wife* a widow. May his children be wandering beggars; may they be driven from their ruined homes. May a creditor seize all he has; may strangers plunder the fruits of his labor. May no one extend kindness to him or take pity on his fatherless children. May his descendants be cut off, their names blotted out from the next generation. May the iniquity of his fathers be remembered before the Lord; may the sin of his mother never be blotted out. May their sins always remain before the Lord, that He may cut off the memory of them from the earth."

The severity of the judgment on Judas and his family makes us shudder. It is very difficult to think of his family having to suffer for what he did. But what Judas had been doing, unwilling to wait for the Lord to decide to exercise His great power as a triumphant Messiah, was building an elaborate home – an *epaulis*. In the Old Testament and the New Testament an epaulis, as a place for human residence, had an inner open courtyard with living quarters built all around it. It would not be a cramped, baked mud brick structure with no private yard such as was so common in the towns and cities of that day. The cost to have such an elaborate home would be considerable. So all of Judas' family, Simon, his father, and his wife and children had to know that Judas was getting money from somewhere to pay for his 'epaulis.' I'm sure they knew he was the treasurer for the twelve. It shouldn't have been hard for them to put two and two together. The implication is they approved or were at least silent.

In Judas' mind, once Jesus restored the kingdom, he and all of the twelve would be in tall clover and would be in charge of Jerusalem, to say nothing about other towns in the nation. Didn't everybody know how rich Solomon and his officials became and how they gave orders to people to get what the officials wanted? Why couldn't he help himself to the money bag in anticipation? If only Jesus would stop fiddling around and do what God had sent Him to do, they could get the show on the road; then he and the other disciples would be directing the affairs of the nation and he could pay back the bag.

As to the severity of the judgment on Judas and his family, consider a sobering example of sin being charged not to just the person who sinned but to his entire family. This is in regard to the destruction of Jericho when Israel entered the Promised Land to drive out all the Canaanite nations. The Israelites were ordered to regard everything in Jericho as devoted to the Lord: "The city and all that was in it was to be devoted to the Lord. Only Rahab the prostitute and all who are with her in her house would be spared, because she hid the spies sent to check out the city. Joshua warned them to keep away from the devoted things, so they would not bring about their own destruction by taking any of them. Otherwise they would make the camp of Israel liable to destruction and bring trouble on it. All the silver and gold and the articles of bronze and iron were declared sacred to the Lord and must go into His treasury." (Joshua 6:19) That seems plain on its face, doesn't it? Let's look at Joshua 7:1: "But the Israelites acted unfaithfully in regard to the devoted things; Achan son of Carmi, the son of Zimri, the son of Zerah, of the tribe of Judah, took some of them. So the Lord's anger burned against Israel." Notice that the scriptures say *the Israelites*, not *someone*, acted unfaithfully. Also that the Lord's anger burned against *Israel*, not against a particular person. Following the destruction of Jericho, Joshua sent a small force of men against Ai, a small town near Jericho with relatively few fighting men, expecting there would be no problem capturing such a town. However, in the attack, they were soundly defeated by a much smaller force. Check out Joshua 7:6: "Then Joshua tore his clothes and fell facedown to the ground before the ark of the Lord, remaining there till evening. The elders of Israel did the same, and sprinkled dust on their heads." Joshua complained to the Lord and questioned His judgment. At that point God issued an ultimatum found in Joshua 7:10-12: "Stand Up! What are you doing down on your face? Israel has sinned; they have violated my covenant, which I commanded them to keep. They have taken some of the devoted things; they have stolen, they have lied, they have put them with their own possessions. That is why the Israelites cannot stand against their enemies; they turn their backs and run because they have been made liable to destruction. I will not be with you anymore unless you destroy whatever among you is devoted to destruction." Joshua 7:15: "He who is caught with the devoted things shall be destroyed by fire, along with all that belongs to him. He has violated the covenant of the Lord and has done a disgraceful thing in Israel."

God was holding all twelve tribes responsible for stealing some of the devoted things. It was imperative that all Israel understand its status as one of solidarity. The word 'they' is mentioned eight times in this account. Following God's direction to Joshua in searching for the person who stole the devoted items,

Achan, of the tribe of Judah, confessed he had committed the sin: "Achan replied, 'It is true! I have sinned against the Lord, the God of Israel. This is what I have done; When I saw in the plunder a beautiful robe from Babylonia, two hundred shekels of silver and a wedge of gold weighing fifty shekels, I coveted them and took them. They are hidden in the ground inside my tent, with the silver underneath.' Then Joshua, together with all Israel, took Achan son of Zerah, the silver, the robe, the gold wedge, his sons and daughters, his cattle, donkeys, and sheep, his tent and all that he had, to the Valley of Achor." (Joshua 7:20-24) Achor means trouble.

Notice how the scripture makes a point of listing everything that belonged to Achan, including all his family and animals. We are then informed in verses 25 and 26 that all Israel stoned him including his sons and daughters and all his animals. "Then all Israel stoned him and after stoning the rest, they burned them. Over Achan they heaped up a large pile of rocks." Why was all of Achan's family put to death? Think about where Achan hid the plunder he took: in a hole in the ground *within his own tent*. How could he have done that without his family knowing it? But no one in his family objected or disclosed his sin to anyone else, thus becoming guilty along with Achan.

With this sobering incident in mind, look again at Psalm 109:16-20: "For he never thought of doing a kindness, but hounded to death the poor and the needy and the brokenhearted. He loved to pronounce a curse–may it come on him, he found no pleasure in blessing–may it be far from him. He wore cursing as his garment; it entered into his body like water, into his bones like oil. May it be like a cloak wrapped about him. May this be the Lord's payment to my accusers, to those who speak evil of me."

Why would Judas be said to hound to death the poor, the needy, the brokenhearted, and in that context, love to pronounce a curse? The phrase 'hound to death' is an obvious exaggeration but what was it that Judas was doing to be tabbed with such an epithet? Remember that Judas was greedy and had his heart set on getting and keeping for his own personal use as much money as he could. Looking at the possibilities of getting more money for the money bag (and thus for himself), Judas must often have privately approached people whom Jesus had recently healed or freed from demon possession, asking for donations to the 'cause.' It would have been hard for them to say no. And even though some happened to be poor or brokenhearted, if they did not give him anything, Judas pronounced a curse on them. He was not sympathetic with the plight of anyone nor did it enter his head to show them any kindness.

Now consider how the Lord spoke of His own plight just before and during His crucifixion. "But you, O Sovereign Lord, deal well with me for your name's sake; out of the goodness of your love, deliver me. For I am poor and needy, and my heart is wounded within me. I fade away like an evening shadow; I am shaken off like a locust. My knees give way from fasting; my body is thin and gaunt. I am an object of scorn to my accusers; when they see me, they shake their heads." (Psalm 109:21-25)

Jesus had been given nothing to eat or drink since the evening meal the day before. He had been bound when arrested. None of his captors, especially the chief priests and elders of the people, had any concern for his physical discomfort. Rather they treated Him with complete contempt, as though He was just an annoying locust to be brushed off into the dust. He had been given no chance to sleep and was time after time slapped or spat upon. He had been blindfolded and struck and mockingly ordered to tell who had hit Him, the implication being that, if He was who He claimed, He would know. When He said His heart was wounded within, we can well understand. His treatment was devastating. His knees were so weak He could not use them to lift His body on the tree enough to breathe better, difficult at best in crucifixion.

It is admittedly difficult to know exactly why and when Judas became a betrayer of his best boyhood friend. We can conjecture, but dogmatism would not be appropriate. It is evident that Satan had full access to Judas during the Lord's public ministry. Jesus described him as being a devil. What we know for sure is that the scripture about Judas was fulfilled and that it would have been better for him to have never been born.

We also know that Satan's chief weapon, then and now, is *deceit*. He is tabbed in the book of Revelation as one "who deceives the whole world." (see Revelation 12:9) Also, "He seized the dragon, that ancient serpent, who is the devil, or Satan, and bound him a thousand years. He threw him into the abyss, and locked and sealed it over him, to keep him from *deceiving the nations* anymore until the thousand years were ended." (Revelation 20:1-3, *emphasis mine)* But when Satan entered Judas at the time of the last meal Jesus shared with the twelve before His death, it is clear Satan had complete control over Judas. Nowhere else is it simply stated 'he entered him' without so much as a 'may I.'

Judas wanted Jesus to be a great king, like David, with a kingdom honored and respected by other nations. For Jesus to be put to death would end his hope of occupying an authoritative position in the kingdom with a conspicuous villa, servants, and anything else he might want.

On the other hand Satan wanted Jesus to die! This would clear the way for him to continue to control the whole world by his deceitful, cunning ways. Neither Judas nor Satan came close to realizing the significance of Jesus' death. In Judas' mind, Jesus' arrest would galvanize Him into establishing His Kingdom without further delay. To Satan, His arrest would lead to His death and would mean the collapse of God's kingdom against his own kingdom. Here we are watching the parade example of Satan's deceit: that of Judas himself, who, caught up in his love of money and things, was easy prey for Satan and useful to him in getting Jesus arrested. How ironic that Satan, eager to devastate His mission, failed to realize Jesus' death would end his existence as prince of the world and result in his eternal condemnation. John 16:8, 11: "When He comes He will convict the world of guilt in regard to sin and righteousness and judgment...in regard to judgment, because the prince of this world now stands condemned."

Having this example before us should be a warning. Anyone who sees life as consisting of attaining things and feathering his own nest opens the door for Satan to enter. First John 2:15-17 puts this problem in a nutshell: "Do not love the world or anything in the world. If anyone loves the world, the love of the Father is not in him. For everything in the world – the cravings of sinful man, the lust of his eyes and the boasting of what he has and does – comes not from the Father but from the world. The world and its desires pass away, but the man who does the will of God lives forever."

"This is what Jesus said, 'Man, who appointed me a judge or an arbiter between you?' Then He said to them, 'Watch out! Be on your guard against all kind of greed; a man's life does not consist in the abundance of his possessions.'" (Luke 12:14-15) Then He added, as part of a parable He told, "But God said to him, 'You fool! This very night your life will be demanded from you. Then who will get what you have prepared for yourself?' This is how it will be with anyone who stores up things for himself but is not rich toward God." (Luke 12:20-21)

CHAPTER 8

The King and His Kingdom in Charge

Just before Jesus began His public ministry, He was led by the Holy Spirit, into the desert to be tempted by an unholy spirit, Satan himself. "Then Jesus was led by the Spirit into the desert to be tempted by the devil. After fasting forty days and forty nights, He was hungry." (Matthew 4:1-2) Also Luke 4:1-2: "Jesus, full of the Holy Spirit, returned from the Jordan and was led by the Spirit in the desert, where for forty days He was tempted by the devil. He ate nothing during those days, and at the end of them He was hungry." (Apparently water was available.)

Satan was well aware that Jesus had a special relationship with God. In Luke 4:3 Satan said to Him, "If you are the Son of God, tell this stone to become bread." Satan's intent was to persuade Jesus to put His own needs for food ahead of the needs of others and thus compromise his ministry of service to others. Mark 10:45: "For even the Son of Man did not come to be served, but to serve, and give His life as a ransom for many." Matthew 20:27-28: "And whoever wants to be first must be your slave – just as the Son of Man did not come to be served, but to serve, and to give His life as a ransom for many."

Jesus' reply was brief but profound, "It is written: man does not live on bread alone." (Matthew 4:4) This is a quote from Deuteronomy 8:3: "Man does not live on bread [food] alone, but on every word that comes from the mouth of God."

It should not be surprising that Satan would tempt Jesus in the matter of eating. In doing so with Adam and Eve in the Garden of Eden, he gained control of all the earthly kingdoms of men. Satan approached Jesus in the desert and may have thought he could also compromise Jesus' ministry to the extent that he could continue to rule the earth he had seized from Adam. Just one example of Jesus accepting Satan's suggestion would destroy the Lord's mission and thwart God's redemptive plan for man.

Jesus' reply to Satan demonstrates how imperative it is for us to know the scriptures and respond only to the Holy Spirit to empower us for service in the kingdom of God.

After Jesus makes this point, Satan gets the point. He takes Jesus to the highest point of the temple and tries to use the scripture to prompt the Lord to jump off, calling attention to Himself in a spectacular display of His power. Satan quotes scripture to justify this! It is important for us today to realize that Satan not only did not quote every word in the two verses, leaving out what he was not interested in, but more importantly, he quoted scripture out of context. If this scripture had been debated in a synagogue, Satan's point would probably have been accepted. Now, as then, many scriptures are quoted out of context from many pulpits as too many pastors seek to enhance their own agenda and cherry pick scriptures accordingly. To quote it out of context to Jesus shows Satan knew all the verses in Psalm 91 (1-16) but hoped Jesus would be duped. "If you are the Son of God," he said, "throw yourself down. For it is written: 'He will command His angels concerning you, and they will lift you up in their hands, so that you will not strike your foot against a stone.' Jesus replied that it is also written, 'Do not put the Lord your God to the test.'" (Matthew 4:6-7) The scripture cited by Satan is found in Psalm 91:11-12. Again, the Lord's reply is brief. Jesus refuses to engage with Satan in a 'he said, she said,' argument. Many of us have not learned this lesson yet. 'He said, she said' is a poor substitute for 'it is written.'

If we examine the entire Psalm the context is clear. *Only those who dwell in the shelter provided by God are promised by God they will be unharmed in all their ways.* Look at verses 1 and 2: "He who dwells in the shelter of the Most High will rest in the shadow of the Almighty. I will say of the Lord, 'He is my refuge and my fortress, my God in whom I trust.'" Then refer to verses 9 and 10: "If you make the Most High your dwelling – even the Lord, who is my refuge – then no harm will befall you, no disaster will come near your tent." One who seeks his own glory does not rest in the shadow of the Almighty. One whose God is his glory is not interested in constantly talking about or showing off his own supposed superiority. Satan was in over his head but didn't seem to know it.

In reply the Lord does not lecture Satan on how to use scripture correctly. That would be a waste of time. He replies succinctly, as seen above: "It is also written 'Do not put the Lord your God to the test.'" (quoted from Deuteronomy 6:16) Satan then appeals to God's ultimate plan for His Messiah – to rule over all the kingdoms of men. "Again, the devil took Him to a very high mountain and showed Him all the kingdoms of the world and their splendor. 'All this I will give you, he said, if you will bow down and worship me.'" Jesus said to him, 'Away from me, Satan! For it is written: Worship the Lord your God, and serve Him only.' Then the devil left Him, and angels came and attended Him." (Matthew 4:8-10) Luke, referring to this same temptation, has Satan saying to Jesus, "The devil led Him to a high place and showed Him in an instant all the kingdoms of the world. And he said to Him, 'I will give you all their authority and splendor, for it has been given to me, and I can give it to anyone I want to. So if you worship me, it will all be yours.'" (Luke 4:5-6)

Notice that it only took *an instant for Satan* to show all that the world had to offer – to Jesus or anyone else for that matter. For a comparison with what God will show us, and how long it will take, if we worship Him, see Ephesians 2:6-7: "And God raised us up with Christ and seated us with Him in the heavenly realms in Christ Jesus, in order that in the coming ages He might show the incomparable riches of His grace, expressed in His kindness to us in Christ Jesus." It only takes an *instant* for us to see and realize that the world's splendor is a sordid display of corrupt morality. But we will be enthralled *throughout all the coming ages* as God shows us His kindness to us in Christ! "To Him be glory in the church and in Christ Jesus throughout all generations forever and ever!" (Ephesians 3:21)

Lest we might think that this initial temptation is the end of Satan's opposition to Jesus, consider Luke 4:13: "When the devil had finished all this tempting, he left Him until an opportune time." Observe that the scripture does not say *until God permits further temptation*. Do you realize that Satan did not get God's permission to begin tempting Jesus? He did not need to. Would God send a Messiah to earth whom He could not permit Satan to test or attempt to kill except at certain times in certain limited ways? What had to happen was the sending of a Messiah whom Satan could tempt when and where he pleased and to any extent he chose without saying a word to God.

Satan, in order to test Job, had to receive permission from God to do so. And God Himself called Satan's attention to Job and his blameless life. Satan then said to God, "'But stretch out your hand and strike everything he has, and he will surely curse you to your face.' The Lord said to Satan, 'Very well then, everything he has is in your hands, but on the man himself do not lay a finger.'" (Job 1:11-12)

But with Jesus, God put no limitations on His testing by Satan. So despite Jesus' admonition to Satan not to test God, or in any way attempt to limit or endanger Him or His mission, Satan would not be kept by God from seeking to destroy Jesus in any way possible, nor would he ever be required to stand down in his efforts. In other words, if Satan could manage to bring about the death of Christ, so be it. Jesus was on His own.

Interestingly, this was not the case with Jesus' disciples. See Luke 22:31-32 (*notes mine*): "Simon, Simon, Satan has asked to sift you [plural] as wheat. But I have prayed [requested God] for you [singular], Simon, that your faith may not fail. And when you have turned back, strengthen your brothers." Satan had to *ask* to test the disciples (the eleven). Permission was granted. Jesus knew Simon would not be able to withstand the testing initially, but would repent and come back to full faith in Christ. He directed Simon to then strengthen his brothers, which subsequently happened (see Acts, chapters 1 and 2).

I don't think Judas Iscariot was tested at all at this time. He had already committed himself to Satan through his love of money and desire for personal aggrandizement. Satan already had Judas in his pocket, so to speak. Satan knew he had complete control of what to do with regard to Jesus. A thought for us: If God had such absolute faith in Jesus' integrity, shouldn't you and I love and honor our Savior the same way? And manifest our faith accordingly? Let us stay alert to some of Satan's 'opportune times' in our own lives. It's a good bet that he must get permission from God to test us today, as he had to do to test Jesus' disciples then. Having some knowledge of Satan's schemes will help us stay on the straight path and better understand why, in His public ministry, Jesus is recorded as doing certain things not easily explainable except as evidence of the battle between Jesus and Satan. Ephesians 6:10: "Finally, be strong in the Lord and in His mighty power. Put on the full armor of God so that you can take your stand against the devil's schemes." Second Corinthians 4:4: "The god of this age has blinded the minds of unbelievers, so that they cannot see the light of the gospel of the glory of Christ, who is the image of God." Second Corinthians 11:3: "But I am afraid that just as Eve was deceived by the serpent's cunning, your minds may somehow be led astray from your sincere and pure devotion to Christ."

So then let's now turn our attention to the Lord's public ministry and observe the instructions Jesus gave His disciples when He selected them to help Him proclaim the gospel to the Jewish nation. "He called His twelve disciples to Him and gave them authority to drive out evil spirits and to heal every disease and sickness." (Matthew 10:1) "These twelve Jesus sent out with the following instructions: 'Do not go among the Gentiles or enter any towns of the Samaritans. Go rather to the lost sheep of Israel. As you go, preach this message: The kingdom of heaven is near. Heal the sick, raise the dead, cleanse those who have leprosy, drive out demons. Freely you have received, freely give. Do not take along any gold or silver or copper in your belts; take no bag for the journey, or extra tunic, or sandals or a staff; for the worker is worth his keep.'" (Matthew 10:5-11) Luke 9:1-2 says essentially the same thing, adding that Jesus gave them power and authority to drive out *all* demons, telling them to preach the kingdom of God and to heal the sick. Settle down in your seats, for this is going to be a battle to the finish between the Kingdom of God and the kingdom of Satan. The Kingdom of God is fully present, just as Satan's. No quarter will be asked or given.

Observe that Jesus had no time for demons nor did He engage them in conversation. Without exception every demon He encountered He ordered to leave those whom they possessed. Although the scripture never says that all demons knew who Jesus was, it seems obvious this was the case. We have no record He ever met one who did not know who He was. Why was this the case? They had been informed about Jesus by Satan himself, whose kingdom was made up of disobedient angels who, by Satanic example and influence, had rebelled against God. Revelation 12:7-8: "And there was war in heaven. Michael and his angels fought against the dragon, and the dragon and his angels fought back. But he was not strong enough, and they lost their place in heaven."

These angels were thrown out of heaven along with Satan. When they left their habitation, they were also deprived of the bodies they had in heaven, thereafter roaming around on earth as unclean disembodied spirits, looking for humans to provide them with bodies or homes. Matthew 12:43-45: "When an evil spirit comes out of a man, it goes through arid places seeking rest and does not find it. Then it says, 'I will return to the house I left.' When it arrives, it finds the house unoccupied, swept clean and put in order. Then it goes and takes with it seven other spirits more wicked than itself, and they go in and live there. And the final condition of that man is worse than the first. That is how it will be with this wicked generation." When demons were confronted by Jesus, they routinely shouted out that He was the Son of God. The Lord always ordered them to be silent, precisely because they knew He was the Son of the Most High God. Demons, by the way, were the first ones in the New Testament to call Jesus the Son of the Most High God beginning with Gabriel's announcement of Jesus' birth. The demons had found out just how high when Satan attempted to take God's place. The demons usually shouted out His identity when they encountered Jesus, lending more credence to the people's idea that God's Messiah had arrived and would be a conquering King. How could a suffering servant cast out demons and why would he want to do so?

To mute this common expectation, Jesus always called Himself the Son of Man. When the people of

Israel thought about the One God anointed to be His Messiah, they expected a Messiah who would rule like David. No one connected a triumphant king, which they wanted, with a suffering servant which they did not want and could not imagine the Messiah to be. So to avoid further misunderstanding, and to discourage any attempt by the people to make Him a king, Jesus ordered the demons He cast out to be silent. Mark 1:32-34: "That evening after sunset the people brought to Jesus all the sick and demon possessed. The whole town gathered at the door, and Jesus healed many who had various diseases. He also drove out many demons, but He would not let the demons speak because they knew who He was." See also Mark 3:11-12. No demon ever called Jesus the 'Son of Man.' This was a term none of the people understood, but it discouraged them from expecting someone like David to restore the kingdom to Israel. Acts 1:3: "After His suffering, He showed himself to these men and gave many convincing proofs that He was alive. He appeared to them over a period of forty days and spoke about the kingdom of God."

Acts 1:6-8: "So when they met together, they asked Him, 'Lord, are you at this time going to restore the kingdom to Israel?' He said to them: 'It is not for you to know the times or dates the Father has set by His own authority. But you will receive power when the Holy Spirit comes on you, and you will be my witnesses in Jerusalem, and in all Judea and Samaria, and to the ends of the earth." It is interesting that those empowered by the unclean spirits were ordered to keep silent about His identity, and those empowered by the Holy Spirit instructed to be His witnesses to the ends of the earth.

When the disciples asked Jesus after His resurrection if He was going to restore the kingdom to Israel at that time, it reveals to us what a major misunderstanding His disciples had about the kingdom even after He rose back to life. The chief priests and the scribes, along with the elders of the people, also completely misunderstood the Kingdom of God. Imagine attributing to the kingdom of Satan what only the Kingdom of God could do. They could not overlook the fact that Jesus did cast out demons but they said he could do so only by Beelzebub, the prince of demons. The Lord's response to this charge is remarkable for the insight it provides. Matthew 12:25-28: "Jesus knew their thoughts and said to them, 'Every kingdom divided against itself will be ruined, and every city or household divided against itself will not stand. If Satan drives out Satan, he is divided against himself. How then can his kingdom stand? And if I drive out demons by Beelzebub, by whom do your people [students] drive them out? So then, they will be your judges. But if I drive out demons by the Spirit [finger] of God, then the kingdom of God has come upon you." Luke 11:20: "But if I drive out demons by the finger of God, then the kingdom of God has come to you." Luke 17:20-21: "Once, having been asked by the Pharisees when the kingdom of God would come, Jesus replied, 'The kingdom of God does not come with your careful observation, nor will people say, 'Here it is,' or 'there it is,' because the kingdom of God is within you.'" There were to be no parades to announce the arrival of the kingdom.

Based on these comments by Jesus, it becomes clear that when Jesus was healing the sick, causing the blind to see, making the lame walk, the kingdom was in full view, as to its power and presence, through the things Jesus was doing.

Even John, the Lord's forerunner, did not understand the nature of the kingdom. "When John heard in prison what Christ was doing, he sent his disciples to ask him, 'Are you the one who was to come, or should we expect someone else?'" (Matthew 11:2) This is the man who saw the Holy Spirit descend and remain on Jesus and heard God voice His approval of His Son! Jesus sent them back to John to report what He had been doing, with the sobering warning that the good news was being preached to the poor and blessed is the one who does not fall away because of Him.

John may have often wondered why Jesus made no attempt to free him from prison. After all, he was the one who introduced Jesus to Israel. When John's disciples had left, Jesus spoke about John and the kingdom to the crowd. Matthew 11:11: "I tell you the truth: among those born of women there has not risen anyone greater than John the Baptist; yet he who is least in the kingdom of heaven is greater than he." John was the last of the prophets before the Kingdom arrived. And all Christians who are reading this are greater than John by virtue of being in the Kingdom of God! So says the Lord. Did you know this about yourself?

What was John's expectation then about the Kingdom of God? Matthew and Luke provide this information. Matthew 3:7-10: "But when he (John) saw many of the Pharisees and Sadducees coming to where he was baptizing, he said to them: 'You brood of vipers! Who warned you to flee from the coming wrath? Produce fruit in keeping with repentance. And do not think you can say to yourselves, 'We have Abraham as our father.' I tell you that out of these stones God can raise up children for Abraham. The ax is laid already at the root of the trees, and every tree that does not produce good fruit will be cut down and thrown into the fire.'" Matthew 3:12: "His (Jesus) winnowing fork is in His hand, and he will clear His threshing floor, gathering His wheat into the barn and burning up the chaff with unquenchable fire." Luke 3:2-3: "During the high priesthood of Annas and Caiaphas, the word of God

131

came to John son of Zechariah in the desert. He went into all the country around the Jordan, preaching a baptism of repentance for the forgiveness of sins."

Given these scriptures, it is somewhat surprising but quite evident that John expected Jesus' ministry to result in immediate judgment for all those who did not repent and show evidence of it in their daily lives. "The ax is already at the root of the trees." "His winnowing fork is [not will be] in His hand." "He will clear His threshing floor." This happens after the wheat is threshed. "He will burn up the chaff with unquenchable fire."

John means business. He does not see Jesus' ministry as love in action, seeking reconciliation in a world of darkness, but as God sending His Son to immediately judge an unbelieving world because it had rejected the light, but God's intent is mirrored in John 3:16-17: "For God so loved the world that He gave His one and only Son, that whoever believes in Him shall not perish but have eternal life. For God did not send His Son into the world to condemn the world, but to save the world through Him."

John had heard about Jesus healing the sick, cleansing the lepers, giving sight to the blind, speech to the dumb, and casting out demons. To John, Jesus had been healing all these people regardless of the way they had been living. John had insisted that those who came to him for baptism had to first repent of their sin and live like it. Jesus, knowing this about John, admonished his disciples, when they returned to John who was in prison at the time, to remind him that the *gospel was being preached to the poor.*

This phrase is found in the Old Testament in Isaiah 61:1: "The Spirit of the Sovereign Lord is on me, because the Lord has anointed me to preach good news to the poor." John certainly would have known this scripture. His own calling came from Isaiah 40:3. If we read further in Isaiah, chapter 60 about Jesus, we find these words, "He has sent me to bind up the brokenhearted, to proclaim freedom for the captives and release from darkness for the prisoners, to proclaim the *year* of the Lord's favor and the *day* of vengeance of our Lord." (*emphasis mine*)

What John may have overlooked was the time difference between "to proclaim the year of the Lord's favor" and the following phrase "and the day of vengeance of our God." John may have assumed both phrases were being used to depict a single event. However, the first phrase refers only to the Lord's public ministry as God's Messiah, the Christ. This is spoken of as the *year of the Lord's favor, not vengeance.* The second phrase refers to a later and completely different time when God will execute judgment on unbelievers. This will not require a *year* to accomplish. When the books are opened and those not written in the Lamb's book of life are judged, the amount of time required for this judgment is not mentioned, indicating it is the 'what' and 'when' not 'how long' that is significant. Revelation 20:12: "And I saw the dead, great and small, standing before the throne, and the books were opened. Another book was opened, which is the book of life." The dead were judged according to what they had done as recorded in the books.

As unlikely as it might seem, no one at the time of His public ministry really understood that Jesus would have to be the sacrifice for the sins of the world and that God would have to strike His Son as though He were sin itself, if the world was to be reconciled to God. Second Corinthians 5:17-19, 21: "Therefore, if anyone is in Christ, he is a new creation; the old has gone the new has come! All this is from God, who reconciled us to Himself through Christ and gave us the ministry of reconciliation; that God was reconciling the world to Himself in Christ, not counting men's sins against them. God made Him who had no sin to be sin for us, so that in Him we might become the righteousness of God." Referring to John again, it would not have been reasonable for Jesus to put the ax to the tree even while He was engaging in a ministry of reconciliation. Wrath (judgment) and reconciliation are not compatible.

Let us continue to focus our attention on the Lord's ministry in light of Satan's opposition and attempts to destroy Him. God will allow Satan to oppose Christ and will place no restrictions on him. This is a must. God must have a Messiah who can successfully resist every temptation and thwart every effort by Satan to destroy Him without interference from God. Christ was ultimately victorious, having defeated Satan on all counts. John 16:8-11: "When He [the Holy Spirit] comes, He will convict the world of guilt in regard to sin and righteousness and judgment: in regard to sin, because men do not believe in me; in regard to righteousness, because I am going to the Father, where you can see me no longer; and in regard to judgment, because the prince of this world now stands condemned."

Given our assessment above of Satan's opposition to the Messiah, let's pick up Jesus' ministry as described in Matthew 4:23-25: "Jesus went throughout Galilee, teaching in their synagogues, preaching the good news of the kingdom, and healing every disease and sickness among the people. News about Him spread all over Syria, and people brought to Him all who were ill with various diseases, those suffering severe pain, the demon possessed, those having seizures, and the paralyzed, and He healed them. Large crowds from Galilee, the Decapolis, Jerusalem, Judea and the region across the Jordan followed Him." On one occasion, when Jesus and his disciples were at Peter's house in Capernaum, the scripture tells us, "When evening came, many who were demon possessed were brought to Him, and He drove out the spirits with a word and healed all the sick. This was to fulfill what was spoken through the prophet Isaiah: 'He took up our infirmities and carried our diseases.'" (Isaiah 53:4)

Matthew now describes Satan's first attempt to kill Jesus. When Jesus saw the crowd around Him, He gave orders to cross to the other side of the lake." (Matthew 8:16-18)

Notice that Jesus did not say why He had decided to cross the lake. Matthew tells us He made this decision when He saw the crowd around Him. Some commentators think it was to get away from the crowd and/or provide rest for himself and His disciples. This same incident is recorded in the other two synoptics, Mark 4:35-36 and Luke 8:22. None of the three give a clear reason for crossing the lake. Mark mentions leaving the crowd behind and Luke, who usually gives less detail than Matthew and Mark, does not mention the presence of a crowd at all. So, unless just getting away from the crowd is, in fact, the reason for the crossing, we would be left in the dark as to why until we are told about what happened out on the lake during the crossing and on shore once across.

Once on the other side Jesus will be in the northern area of the Decapolis, a large region of ten cities (and probably other smaller villages) on the east side of the Jordan and populated mostly by Gentiles. Jesus had never gone to the Decapolis before, but some people from the Decapolis had been to Galilee to see and hear the man who casts out demons and heals the sick. Jesus Himself had never been in that region of the Decapolis which Satan had on lockdown.

While Jesus and the disciples were out on the lake crossing over, a furious storm came up on the lake and waves swept over the boat. Jesus was sleeping. "The disciples went and woke Him, saying, 'Lord save us! We're going to drown!' He replied, 'You of little faith, why are you so afraid?' Then He got up and rebuked the winds and the waves and it was completely calm." (Matthew 8:25-26)

Some commentators go into a detailed explanation of the reason for the storm, basically attributing it to the lake being several hundred feet below sea level, often causing hot air rising from the lake to draw in and mix with winds coming across the lake from the east or southeast, producing strong squalls with little or no warning. Matthew mentions that this storm happened without warning while the boat was on the way across the lake. Matthew 8:23-25: "Then He got into the boat and His disciples followed Him. Without warning, a furious storm came up on the lake, so that the waves swept over the boat. But Jesus was sleeping. The disciples went and woke Him, saying, 'Lord, save us! We are going to drown!'"

I think this was one of Satan's opportune times, and that he was attempting to sink the boat and drown Jesus and the disciples with Him. Remember how Satan caused a strong wind to collapse a house on Job's children, killing all of them. Satan caused a strong wind to collapse the older son's house after God gave him permission to strike everything Job had. Job 1:19: "When suddenly a mighty wind swept in from the desert and struck the four corners of the house. It collapsed on them and they are dead, and I am the only one who has escaped to tell you."

But Satan did not have to ask permission from God to cause this storm in hopes of sinking the boat and drowning all on board. No holds were barred from Satan. Jesus was on His own. The rest of the story will nail this down. After the disciples woke up Jesus, He ordered the wind and waves to subside and the lake became calm. Matthew 8:26-27: "He replied, 'You of little faith, why are you so afraid?' Then He got up and rebuked the winds and the waves, and it was completely calm." The question is, why did Jesus chide them over their lack of faith? He did this *before* He rebuked the winds and waves. Mark 4:40 states

"Do you still have no faith?" Luke put it this way: "Where is your faith?" We may hesitate to think that Jesus was disappointed because the disciples did not order the storm to cease, but apparently that is what He expected of them. The synoptic records make it clear that Jesus, during His public ministry, chided His disciples more for their lack of faith than for any other failing on their part.

Jesus really got excited when He observed someone trusting Him implicitly. Matthew 8:5-8: "When Jesus had entered Capernaum, a centurion came to Him, asking for help. 'Lord,' he said, 'my servant lies at home paralyzed and in terrible suffering.' Jesus said to him, 'I will go and heal him.' The centurion replied, 'Lord, I do not deserve to have you come under my roof. But just say the word, and my servant will be healed.'" Matthew 8:10,13: "When Jesus heard this He was astonished and said to those following Him, 'I tell you the truth, I have not found anyone in Israel with such great faith.' Then Jesus said to the centurion, 'Go! It will be done just as you believed it would.'" Guess what? The centurion was a gentile!

Matthew 15:22,25-28: "A Canaanite woman from that vicinity [Tyre and Sidon], crying out 'Lord, Son of David, have mercy on me! My daughter is suffering terribly from demon possession.' The woman came and knelt before Him, 'Lord, help me,' she said. He replied, 'It is not right to take the children's bread and give it to their dogs.' 'Yes, Lord,' she said, 'but even the dogs eat the crumbs that fall from their masters' table.' Then Jesus answered, 'Woman, you have great faith! Your request is granted.' And her daughter was healed from that very hour." Nowhere in the Gospels does Jesus commend any of His disciples, nor any Jew for that matter, for having strong faith.

Now when their boat, having weathered the storm, reached the other side of the lake in the region of the Gadarenes, two demon possessed men met Him. Why did they do this? The answer is found in a fascinating account of Satan's attempt to keep Jesus out of his territory, ending with complete victory for Jesus. This account is recorded in all three of the synoptics, to which we now turn. Matthew 8:28-31: "When He arrived at the other side in the region of the Gadarenes, two demon possessed men coming from the tombs met Him. They were so violent that no one could pass that way. 'What do you want with us, Son of God?' they shouted! 'Have you come here to torture us before the appointed time?' Some distance away from them a large herd of pigs was feeding. The demons begged Jesus, 'If you drive us out, send us into the herd of pigs.'"

Mark 5:1-10: "They went across the lake to the region of the Gerasenes. When Jesus got out of the boat, a man with an evil spirit came from the tombs to meet Him. This man lived in the tombs, and no one could bind him any more, not even with a chain. For he had often been chained hand and foot, but he tore the chains apart and broke the irons on his feet. No one was strong enough to subdue him. Night and day among the tombs and in the hills he would cry out and cut himself with stones. When he saw Jesus from a distance, he ran and fell on his knees in front of Him. He shouted at the top of his voice, 'What do you want with me, Jesus, Son of the Most High God? Swear to me that you won't torture me!' For Jesus had said to him, 'Come out of this man, you evil spirit!' Then Jesus asked him, 'What is your name?' 'My name is Legion,' he replied, 'for we are many.' And he begged Jesus again and again not to send them out of the area. A large herd of pigs was feeding on a nearby hillside. The demons begged Jesus, 'Send us among the pigs, allow us to go into them.'"

Luke 8:27-32: "When Jesus stepped ashore, he was met by a demon possessed man from the town. For a long time this man had not worn clothes or lived in a house, but had lived in the tombs. When he saw Jesus, he cried out and fell at His feet, shouting at the top of his voice, 'What do you want with me, Jesus, Son of the Most High God? I beg you, don't torture me!' For Jesus had commanded the evil spirit to come out of the man. Many times it had seized him, and though he was chained hand and foot and kept under guard, he had broken his chains and had been driven by the demon into solitary places. Jesus asked him, 'What is your name?' 'Legion,' he replied, because many demons had gone into him. And they begged Him repeatedly not to order them to go into the abyss. A large herd of pigs was feeding there on the hillside. The demons begged Jesus to let them go into them, and He gave them permission." (Luke 8:30-32)

It is clear that the demons were aware Jesus was coming to their area. Luke says that *when Jesus stepped ashore he was met by the demon possessed man*. Mark says that *when Jesus got out of the boat, seeing Jesus from a distance, the man with the evil spirit came from the tombs to meet Him*. Matthew also implies that *the men came on purpose to meet Jesus as soon as he arrived*. Although Matthew mentions *two* men, the account centers on the one driven away from his town and family. There are also differences in the name of the hometown. Three towns or villages with similar names were in close proximity in that part of the Decapolis.

This is the only instance in the New Testament where demons seek to confront Jesus. As noted above, this was Gentile territory. Jews don't herd pigs. Satan had this part of the Decapolis completely under his control. His strategy to remain in charge in that area begins to unfold.

Based on the scriptures just cited, we can be sure Satan wanted to keep Jesus out of the Decapolis. His chance of doing this would be enhanced if he could keep Jesus from establishing a beachhead. It did not matter to Satan and his demons that the demoniac had not been able to go home to be with his family in a long time. Satan was happy when the man snapped his chains and became so violent he could not be allowed to stay at home and was driven to the tombs. Together, these two men terrorized the region where the tombs were, and they were such a threat to others no one dared enter that area.

How then will Satan prevent Jesus from proclaiming the good news of the kingdom in the Decapolis? For the answer, consider the rest of the scriptures dealing with this issue. Matthew 8:32-9:1: "He said to them, 'Go!' So they came out and went into the pigs, and the whole herd rushed down the steep bank into the lake and died in the water. Those tending the pigs ran off, went into the town and reported all this, including what had happened to the demon possessed men. Then the whole town went out to meet Jesus. And when they saw Him, they pleaded with him to leave their region. Jesus stepped into the boat, crossed over and came to his own town. End of the story? Hardly.

143

Hear Mark 5:14-20: "Those tending the pigs ran off and reported this in the town and countryside, and the people went out to see what had happened. When they came to Jesus, they saw the man who had been possessed by the legion of demons, sitting there, dressed and in his right mind; and they were afraid. Those who had seen it told the people what had happened to the demon possessed man – and told about the pigs as well. Then the people began to plead with Jesus to leave their region. As Jesus was getting into the boat, the man who had been demon possessed begged to go with Him. Jesus did not let him, but said, 'Go home to your family and tell them how much the Lord has done for you and how He has had mercy on you.' So the man went away and began to tell in the Decapolis how much Jesus had done for him. And all the people were amazed."

Luke 8:34-39: "When those tending the pigs saw what had happened, they ran off and reported this in the town and countryside, and the people went out to see what had happened. When they came to Jesus, they found the man from whom the demons had gone out, sitting at Jesus feet, dressed and in his right mind, and they were afraid. Those who had seen it told the people how the demon possessed man had been cured. Then all the people of the region of the Gerasenes asked Jesus to leave them, because they were overcome with fear. So He got into the boat and left.

The man from whom the demons had gone out begged to go with Him, but Jesus sent him away, saying, 'Return home and tell how much God has done for you.' So the man went away and told all over town how much Jesus had done for him.''

Before Jesus left Galilee to cross the lake, He must have already heard about the two demonized men who were so violent no one could go through the area where the tombs were. There certainly were no crowds there! His awareness of Satan's control of that area may have prompted His decision to go over to the region and liberate it and the demon possessed men. I think Jesus was greatly affected upon hearing about this situation. Would He have known Satan would oppose His plan to liberate the countryside area around Gadara? I think so, no doubt.

Satan, realizing Jesus would cast out demons in Decapolis as He had been doing in Galilee and would proclaim the kingdom throughout the area, devised a plan to turn the people against Jesus as soon as He arrived in the region. Since it was Jesus' habit to cast out every demon He encountered, Satan would have his demons confront Him, through the man they controlled, and beg to go into the herd of pigs. Satan must have thought that Jesus would like the idea of demons having to be satisfied with living in pigs. There is a bit of humor here, and I can only laugh about demons reduced to asking permission to go into pigs. There is no example in the New Testament of demons asking permission to enter humans, much less animals. We are not told this of course, but Satan might have taken some guff from the legion of demons when they found out they were to beg Jesus to send them into those pigs. I don't think they liked the pigs any better than the Jews did.

At any rate, the demons were to be on the lookout for Christ's arrival and were instructed by Satan to approach Him as soon as he got out of the boat. And when they made this unusual request, guess what? Jesus agreed and simply said, 'Go.' They did, and under the control of the demons the entire herd of pigs rushed into the lake and drowned. Satan had planned for this to happen and knew the owners would be upset when they found out their pigs were dead. Those who had been herding the pigs told everyone about what had happened. Jesus had ordered the demons out of the demon possessed man and allowed them to enter the pigs, promptly driving the pigs into the lake, killing the entire herd. And the man himself, who had been living in the tombs, cutting himself, undressed, shouting day and night, so violent no one could control or approach him, was sitting with Jesus, dressed and in his right mind!

Hearing about all this, the pig owners and the whole town plus many others from the countryside, came out to meet Jesus and plead with Him to leave. The loss of pigs was their concern, not the curing of the man who had the legion of demons. At their insistence, Jesus and the disciples got into their boat and left. It looked like Satan's strategy had worked and he had successfully put one over on the Lord. Satan must have thought: "This is a piece of cake. I won't have to worry any more about Him coming over here."

But just before Jesus got into the boat to leave, the former demoniac asked Jesus if he could go with Him. At first thought, we might have expected Jesus to agree. Instead, Jesus denied his request and told him to go home to his family and tell them of God's mercy to him. So the man went away and *told all over town* how much Jesus had done for him. Mark 5:19-20: "Jesus did not let him, but said, 'Go home to your family and tell them how much the Lord has done for you and how he has had mercy on you.' So the man went away and began to tell *in the Decapolis* how much Jesus had done for him. And all the people were amazed." (*emphasis mine*)

This lays the ground for consideration of this man's background. Let's do that now. What kind of a man would a whole legion of demons (usually several thousand) seek to control and be their home? No one else in the Bible even comes close to having that many demons. Jesus had cast out seven demons from Mary Magdalene (Luke 8:2). The herd of pigs on a hillside nearby numbered about two thousand according to Mark 5:13. There were enough demons to go around.

Apparently this man, before he had become demon possessed had been hard to live with, both by his family and his home town, and under demonic influence, caused so much trouble by his repulsive, reprehensible behavior that he had to be chained and kept under guard. The demon would come and go as it pleased, in effect setting the whole town on edge. Whenever it came, the man was able to break his chains and became progressively more violent. This happened over and over. The demon would also drive him into the desert. Obviously, each time the demon reentered the man it brought other demons to live in him (see Matt. 12:43-45) until finally, driven out of his mind, the man wound up living in the tombs, cut off from his family, naked, cutting himself with rocks and crying out day and night, basically insane, all the while becoming so violent no one could pass that way for fear of his life. Luke 8:29: "For Jesus had commanded the evil spirit to come out of the man. Many times it had seized him, and though he was chained hand and foot and kept under guard, he had broken his chains and had been driven by the demon into solitary places."

As a result of two thousand pigs drowning in the lake and the resultant restoration of the demoniac to his right mind, everyone throughout the Decapolis heard what had happened. The story was told and retold about Jesus, including the curing of the demoniac and the fate of the pigs. Then there was this former demoniac, going throughout the Decapolis telling everyone how and by whom he had been delivered of the legion of demons. "And all the people were amazed" is putting it mildly. (Mark 5:20)

Satan had been willing to concede the loss of one person in order to retain control of the Decapolis. Little did he realize how this one person, liberated from a hopeless condition and known through the entire region for his violence, would proclaim in the entire Decapolis the great compassion and mercy of God.

Satan routinely underestimates Christians who consistently witness for Jesus about His love and grace. No one can fully tell his story except that person himself. People under the influence of Satan hear nothing about God's grace. Satan cannot relate to kindness or compassion. The more destructive he can be in the world, the better.

As you might suspect there is a sequel to this great victory of Jesus over Satan. It begins later on in the Lord's ministry, when Jesus is in Tyre and decides to return to the Decapolis by way of Sidon. Going this way, through Sidon, puts Jesus coming around the north side of the Sea of Galilee (the lake) and proceeding south on the east side of the lake and the Jordan, in a section of the Decapolis not far from the place where the demons drowned all the pigs.

Mark 7:31-32: "Then Jesus left the vicinity of Tyre and went through Sidon, down to the Sea of Galilee and into the region of the Decapolis. There some people brought to him a man who was deaf and could hardly talk, and they begged Him to place His hand on the man." When the man had been healed, Jesus told the people who had brought the man to Jesus not to tell anyone. "Jesus commanded them not to tell anyone. But the more He did so, the more they kept talking about it. People were overwhelmed with amazement. 'He has done everything well,' they said. 'He even makes the deaf hear and the mute speak.'" (Mark 7:36-37) Matthew fills in more of the picture for us. "Jesus left there [Tyre] and went along the Sea of Galilee [the lake]. Then He went up on a mountainside and sat down. Great crowds [of Gentiles] came to Him, bringing the lame, the blind, the crippled, the mute and many others, and laid them at His feet, and He healed them. The people were

150

amazed when they saw the mute speaking, the crippled made well, the lame walking and the blind seeing. [This went on for three days.] And they praised the God of Israel." (Matthew 15:29-31) Had these been Jews, they would not have used the phrase 'the God of Israel.'

Now look at what happened next! "Jesus called his disciples to Him and said, 'I have compassion for these people; they have already been with me three days and have nothing to eat. I do not want to send them away hungry, or they may collapse on the way.' His disciples answered, 'Where could we get enough bread in this remote place to feed such a crowd?' 'How many loaves do you have?' Jesus asked. 'Seven,' they replied, 'and a few small fish.'" (Matthew 15:32-34)

Jesus then proceeded to feed the crowd, multiplying the food on hand. There were four thousand, not counting women and children. Afterward Jesus sent them away, and He and His disciples went by boat (no sudden storm this time) to the vicinity of Magadan, located on the west shore of the lake. (Matthew 15:35-39)

So the Decapolis is now completely open to the good news of the kingdom, the Gentiles having opened their hearts to the God of Israel. And, wonder of wonders, one of the only two times a multitude of people were fed by Christ occurred in Gentile Decapolis! He had compassion on the people and was wonderfully sensitive to their physical needs. Aren't you proud of such a Savior? And does anyone have any doubts that Christ is more than a match for Satan? It's okay if you shout "HOSANNA!"

We will examine one more episode involving the Lord's deliverance of people from demon possession. In Matthew 16:21-22 Jesus tells His disciples (the twelve, in particular) for the first time that He will suffer greatly at the hands of the elders, chief priests and teachers of the law and that He must be killed and on the third day be raised to life. Although this was plain talk, it was completely contrary to their expectations. "He then began to teach them that the Son of Man must suffer many things and be rejected by the elders, chief priests and teachers of the law, and that He must be killed and after three days rise again. He spoke plainly about this, and Peter took Him aside and began to rebuke Him." (Mark 8:31-32) This indicated a complete failure by the twelve to understand what Jesus had revealed to them. Their refusal to accept what the Lord told them about His death also left them in the dark with regard to the Lord's disclosure that He would be raised on the third day. What on earth was He talking about? They were not at all willing to listen to Jesus tell them He was going to be killed. And at this point, He had not revealed His death would be by crucifixion.

This refusal to listen to Jesus led to the Mount of Transfiguration experience where God Himself, clothed in Shekinah Glory, spoke audibly in the presence of Peter, James, John, and Elijah and Moses. God's last three words were, "Listen to Him!" never spoken audibly by God before or since.

The next morning Jesus and the three disciples, Peter, James and John, whom He had taken with Him to be on the mountain so they could hear God confirm what Jesus had told them a week earlier about suffering and dying in Jerusalem, went down the mountain. As they approached the other disciples, a man came to Jesus, very distraught, upset because the disciples could not cast out a demon from his only son. Mark tells us what happened.

"When they came to the other disciples [the nine left at the foot of the mountain], they saw a large crowd around them and the teachers of the law arguing with them. As soon as all the people saw Jesus, they were overwhelmed with wonder and ran to greet Him. 'What are you arguing with them about?' He asked. A man in the crowd answered, 'Teacher, I brought you my son, who is possessed by a spirit that has robbed him of speech. Whenever it seizes him, it throws him to the ground. He foams at the mouth, gnashes his teeth and becomes rigid. I asked your disciples to drive out the spirit, but they could not.' 'O unbelieving generation,' Jesus replied, 'how long shall I stay with you? How long shall I put up with you? Bring the boy to me.' So they brought him. When the spirit saw Jesus, it immediately threw the boy into a convulsion. He fell to the ground and rolled around, foaming at the mouth. Jesus asked the boy's father, 'How long has he been like this?' 'From childhood,' he answered. 'It has often thrown him into fire or water to kill him. But if you can do anything, take pity on us and help us.'"

Please note that Jesus did not address the demon at all until He commanded the spirit to leave. He learns about the nature of this demon from the father's remarks. We learn from Luke's account that the boy is an only son, and from both Luke and Matthew we get terse statements of his healing, "Jesus rebuked the demon, and it came out of the boy." (Matthew 17:18) Luke 9:42-43 is better but brief: "Even while the boy was coming, the demon threw him to the ground in a convulsion. But Jesus rebuked the evil spirit, healed the boy and gave him back to his father. And they were all amazed at the greatness of God."

It remains for Mark to give us exactly what Jesus said, and why, when He cast out the demon. "When Jesus saw that a crowd was running to the scene, He rebuked the evil spirit. 'You deaf and mute spirit,' he said, 'I command you, come out of him and never enter him again.' The spirit shrieked, convulsed him violently and came out. The boy looked so much like a corpse that many said, 'He's dead.' But Jesus took him by the hand and lifted him to his feet, and he stood up." (Mark 9:25-27)

Now comes the question from the disciples who tried, but couldn't cast out the demon. "Why couldn't we drive it out?" (Mark 9:28) The answer to this question also intrigued those who copied the early manuscripts. They apparently did not know either why the disciples failed. Those who were employed to reproduce the manuscripts of the Bible, many of them monks in monasteries, must themselves have had a love for their work. I think we can be assured they made every effort to copy each manuscript faithfully and without error. But as they copied the manuscripts, they themselves had different ideas about the disciples' failure. A number of them, in an effort to be helpful, often placed their own ideas out on the side of the page they happened to be copying. Some seemed to be quite confident they knew why the disciples were unable to get rid of the demon in the lad. As would be expected, the results of all these helpful efforts led to manuscripts with different wording. We don't really know how many transcribers were at work diligently copying the available manuscripts, but it has been relatively easy to sort them into different families of manuscripts based on which copyists usually made which mistakes. As an example, one group of copyists often repeated the last word in a sentence as the first word in the next sentence. Others commonly misspelled the same word. Many manuscripts were copied by scribes listening to a manuscript being read by someone, making it harder to spell and copy correctly. This is just a brief excerpt about the problem of accuracy and does not bring us the answer to the disciples' question: why couldn't we cast out that demon? So let's go to Jesus for the answer, then return to what some of our copyists thought.

Mark 9:25-26: "When Jesus saw that a crowd was running to the scene, He rebuked the evil spirit. 'You deaf and mute spirit,' He said, 'I command you, come out of him and never enter him again.' The spirit shrieked, convulsed him violently and came out." The demon simply *did not hear* the disciples order it to leave the boy. Look at what Jesus called it – a *deaf and mute* spirit. How did Jesus know the spirit was mute? The boy's father told Him. "Teacher, I brought you my son, who is possessed by a spirit that has robbed him of speech." (Mark 9:17) Why did Jesus tell the demon never to enter him again? We have no record of Jesus saying that to any other demon. The father told Jesus it had often entered his son. This demon, unable to speak, liked to announce his presence by throwing the boy around and shrieking loudly. But the father said nothing about the demon depriving the boy of hearing. How then did Jesus know the demon was also deaf?

Many today say Jesus knows everything, period. If that were true, then why did Jesus ask so many questions throughout His public ministry? He asked the father how long his son had been possessed. "How long has he been like this?" (Mark 9:21) *Jesus knew the demon was deaf simply because it did not obey the disciples' order to leave.* Jesus had already given His disciples authority and power over *all* demons. (Luke 9:1) This was the first time they had encountered a deaf demon.

Did Jesus blame them for their failure? Yes, He did. When they were together, away from the crowd, they asked Jesus why they couldn't drive out the demon. "Jesus replied, 'Because you have so little faith. I tell you the truth, if you have faith as small as a mustard seed, you can say to this mountain, 'Move from here to there, and it will move. Nothing will be impossible for you.'" (Matthew 17:19-21) The most accurate manuscripts do not have a verse 21.

The King James Version adds a verse 21, "Howbeit this kind goeth not out but by prayer and fasting." The most likely reason for this verse is a scribal attempt to answer the disciples' question. The scribes who included this in the scripture they were copying seem not to have realized Jesus did not teach His disciples to fast. In fact, the Pharisees' disciples and those of John the Baptist wondered why Jesus did not teach his disciples to fast. "Now John's disciples and the Pharisees were fasting. Some people came and asked Jesus, 'How is it that John's disciples and the disciples of the Pharisees are fasting, but yours are not?' Jesus answered, 'How can the guests of the bridegroom fast while he is with them? They cannot, so long as they have him with them. But the time will come when the bridegroom will be taken from them, and on that day they will fast.'" (Mark 2:18-20) Jesus was referring to wedding customs of the day and, I think, secondarily to His own departure. Often a week of feasting and fellowship preceded the actual wedding ceremony. This certainly would not be a time for anyone invited to attend to refuse to eat and feast with all the other guests. This would be an insult to the bridegroom who was responsible for seeing there would be food for all those invited. There could be no fasting by anyone until the wedding was over and the bridegroom and his wife and all the guests were gone.

Jesus not only did not teach his disciples to fast, He prohibited them from doing so while He was with them. Some of the scribes who copied Mark also made the same mistake about fasting in Mark 9:29: "He [Jesus] replied, 'This kind can only come out by prayer and fasting.'" The most accurate manuscripts read "This kind can come out only by prayer." Luke does not record the disciples asking Jesus why they had failed.

In further consideration of this matter of fasting, the scribes who inserted it in the manuscripts they copied must have had in mind fasting and prayer as an ongoing way of life. But what did Jesus have in mind when he told his disciples that this kind only comes out by prayer and faith? The disciples had already been out proclaiming the kingdom and casting out demons. "They went out and preached that people should repent. They drove out many demons and anointed many sick people with oil and healed them." (Mark 6:12-13)

But when they were asked to cast out the deaf demon and it did not leave the boy at their command, they did not have enough faith to ask God to order it out. They gave up. This lack of faith kept them from asking God, in Jesus absence, to cast the demon out. This is what Jesus meant when He told them "this kind only goes out by prayer." He was not telling them that they had not been praying enough on a daily basis. If that were the case, then why were they so successful up to that point in casting out demons? Later on, after Jesus had cursed the unfruitful fig tree near Jerusalem, He would tell them that whatever they asked in prayer, believing, they would receive. "Therefore I tell you, whatever you ask for in prayer, believe that you have received it, and it will be yours." (Mark 11:24) Luke, only 6 verses after their failure with the demonized boy, chooses it seems with tongue in check, to further emphasize the disciples inept performance and self-centered attitude. "'Master,' said John, 'we saw a man driving out demons in your name and we tried to stop him, because he is not one of us.' 'Do not stop him,' Jesus said, 'for whoever is not against you is for you.'" (Luke 9:49-51)

I'm sure the Lord was exasperated with the twelve many times. When He came down from the Mount of Transfiguration and found an uproar over the disciples' failure, it provoked Him deeply. "'O unbelieving and perverse generation,' Jesus replied, 'How long shall I stay with you? How long shall I put up with you? Bring the boy here to me.'" Jesus rebuked the demon, and it came out of the boy, and he was healed from that moment. Jesus did not say He was provoked with the crowd, or the father, or the disciples, but with the generation, that is, with all of them, and not just over that episode.

The word 'generation' takes in everyone living in that generation. Luke puts the final touch to a beautiful example of the King and His Kingdom in charge,

"And they were all amazed at the greatness of God." (Luke 9:43)